Port of the Dragon

The Lost Harbor of Sir Francis Drake

Laird L. Nelson

Port of the Dragon. *The Lost Harbor of Sir Francis Drake.*

Revised second printing, September 2015.

ISBN-13: 978-0692282847 (Laird L. Nelson)
ISBN-10: 069228284X

Book and cover design, typography and prepress preparations: Kathleen Weisel, Bellingham, WA (weiselcreative.com)

Editor: Dixie Cheek, Bellingham, WA

Printed through CreateSpace Independent Publishing Platform

Cover: photos by Laird L. Nelson. Detail of 'Jodocus Hondius map of 1589' showing cove in New Albion visited by Francis Drake, sourced from Wikipedia Creative Commons, as were some other interior images. Back cover photo, looking northwest from Chuckanut Drive toward Lummi: Kathleen Weisel.

Web addresses listed in References were sourced between 2005 and 2012.

Dedicated to the local men and women
who sailed north to Alaska in the fishing industry
and never returned.

Contents

FRANCISCVS · 1598 · FRANCISCVS DRACO NOBILISSIMVS ANGLIAE EQVES, REI NAVTICAE AC BELLICAE PERITISSIMVS

AVDENTES FORTV-
NA IVVAT

Cognita Nasoni mea si quoque vita fuisset,
Neptuni vere sobolem narrasset, et alis
Expansis Mundum circumuolitasse per undas,
Flammtuom in mira metamorphosi vsque Draconem
Conuersum fueram semper sic faucibus ipse,
Vnguibus atque alis, caudaq armatus in hostem.

Portrait of Sir Francis Drake 1598 by Crispin de Passe.

....

Introduction

....

A T TIMES ALONG OUR HISTORICAL PATH important events get lost, witnesses die, fire consumes written accounts, or someone hides the truth. The 430-year-old mystery of where English privateer Francis Drake landed on the Northwest Coast of America involves a case of deceit: a cover-up took place from the start and was renewed again 200 years later. Preceded only by the fleet of Magellan, first to sail around the world, Drake covered more of the globe than Magellan when he turned his ships north in the Pacific and entered a hidden sea where no Chinese junks or Russian explorers had ever navigated before.

In the late 16th century, Francis Drake made a daring and profitable three-year voyage around the world. He returned to England with a ship named the *Golden Hind*, loaded with stolen Spanish treasure. Elizabeth I knighted him for his rich accomplishment, but she seized all of his logs, and they were never seen again. All of his crew was sworn to secrecy under penalty of death, and the Queen never allowed any publications of his voyage during her lifetime. But information did leak out. Rumors and theories spread throughout the English court, and piece by piece details started to emerge. Some of Drake's crew broke silence in the *Anonymous Narrative* and revealed important information. Still, they left a host of unanswered questions.

In his long journey across the Atlantic, Drake fought bitter cold, howling storms, and mutiny before passing through the Strait of Magellan into Spanish colonial territory. This bold, determined, at-any-cost buccaneer caught the Spanish off guard, with no military resources in the Pacific. He raided seaport towns, plundered gold and silver, and disrupted Spanish trade from southern Chile to lower Mexico, and then disappeared into the vast Pacific. On course to the west, he then turned north into uncharted waters, where he landed on the Northwest Coast of America in June of 1579.

The clues, from *The World Encompassed 1628* or *The Famous Voyage*, published fifty years after the fact, have misguided historians into thinking he landed in Northern California, just above San Francisco at Point Reyes. But others claim he landed in Oregon, and another that he landed in British Columbia. Modern-day navigators have tried to retrace his Pacific route without success. No bays or islands matched the old writings. So their conclusion is that Drake's astronomical readings were wrong, or the northern part of his voyage never happened.

Now, new discoveries have found that Drake made accurate readings. His calculations for his lost harbor are just six minutes off. However, England employed a cover-up. In doing so, the writers of the time changed his landing by ten degrees. They also changed important phrases in *The World Encompassed 1628* and added misinformation in the footnotes of *The Famous Voyage*. So English deceit from the start, and renewed again in 1792 by Captain George Vancouver, directed historians to the wrong location.

These new discoveries show that Drake landed in North America at N 48°, a latitude documented in both English and Spanish archives. But as stated, the degrees match no bays, because what the first explorers meant is *within* N 48° (between N 48° to N 49°), a distance that spans about 69 miles, where Drake landed in three different bays in the new country he named Nova Albion (New Britain). These three bays lie at different degrees in Northwest Washington State, with his third harbor shown on an old map called the Portus Nove Albionis (the Portus Map).

Why has this English buccaneer stayed alive all these centuries through a multitude of books and articles always projecting a new theory? Why is it even important as to where he landed and spent five weeks working on his two ships?

Rightfully, something about his landing is significant, or at stake, because a couple of historians in California almost came to blows over disagreements about which local bay he landed in. Not a rare occurrence, since at times tempers flare, but besides the conflict these three events are of interest: First, treasure hunters believe he hid Spanish booty somewhere around his lost harbor. Second, historians would like to know where he made first European contact with Native Americans and what happened to a settlement or castaways he left behind. Third, navigators

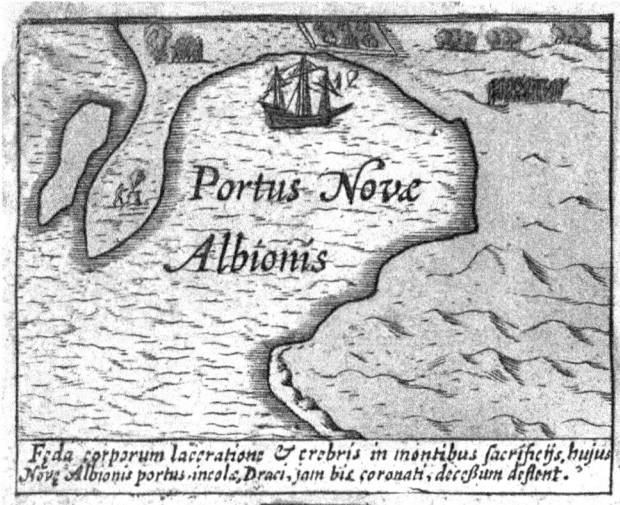

Detail of Jodocus Hondius map of 1589 showing cove in New Albion visited by Francis Drake. Sourced from Wikipedia, public domain.

for sure have an interest in where this gutsy Englishman sailed with his old square rigger.

To answer these questions, take a brief trip through English, Spanish, and early American history. Find out what motivated this famous privateer. Follow his 1577 voyage and see what treasure he stole from the Spanish. Then see what route he took in the Pacific and the bays where he landed in Nova Albion. Before leaving, he set up a monument to claim his new country for England that is still visible today. Observe his monument along with his famous "plate of brass."

Spain, stunned and confused after Drake's raid, were slow to develop a defensive plan. In 1582, they got lucky when they captured Drake's young cousin John, an artist who helped document the famous voyage. With information from John, in 1592, they sent pilot Juan the Greek to search for Drake's North American landing site. While searching, Juan charted the west side of Vancouver Island that runs well into today's Strait of Juan de Fuca. Juan did not find Drake's harbor, although he made an important discovery. Later, in the late 1700's, to honor the old Greek navigator, an English fur trader named this east-west waterway Juan de Fuca from a 200-year-old Michael Loc story. The name the English assigned for this 90-mile-long strait is wrong; no navigator named Fuca ever existed. The correct name is in the English and Spanish archives.

After the voyage of Juan the Greek, a 180-year lull took place and no recorded voyages ventured to the Pacific Northwest. But the politics continued with the fabricated Spanish voyage of Admiral de Fonté.

In the late 1700's came the Spanish voyage of Juan Perez in the *Santiago*. Then English Captain James Cook showed up on his third voyage of exploration, followed by the French, and as a result, fur traders from six different nations started to show up in the Pacific Northwest without a Spanish license. Spain at that time claimed all rights to the Pacific, and the "Nootka Sound Incident" almost sparked war with England. This clash between two powers brought attention to this new country. As a consequence, early explorers started to chart the area, with Spain and England documenting most events for this timeline. But the Spanish hid important information, as did the first English explorers, because they both discovered where Drake landed over 200 years ago. Then why didn't they document it? The Spanish indirectly did and then attempted to cover it up. The English left a trail to follow, but still misguided historians.

What's in a name? Both early English and Spanish explorers only had one way to identify their discoveries: the names they assigned. The problem confronted in the area of where Drake landed is that the names have been changed and then changed again. Some names have been moved to different locations and some names have completely disappeared. So the original names tell a different story than what we know today. Throughout these different timelines all the historical events covered here have been individually documented, but look at the bigger picture and discover how all the pieces fit together, with a missing player, and the lost North American landing of Sir Francis Drake.

While English and Spanish explorers conducted their surveys in the Pacific Northwest, George Washington held the office of president of the United States. But the Americans were on the move from their original colonies. Piece by piece they acquired the country we know today, and in 1841, the Wilkes Expedition, unknowing, charted the area of where Drake landed. At that time, with the English on the north, the Spanish on the south, and Native Americans in the middle, wagon trains rolled

Map of the fabricated Spanish voyage of Admiral de Fonté.

over the Oregon Trail. In settling Drake's new country, smallpox and religion decimated native oral history. Then an American dispute with England over islands Drake named the Islands of Saint James almost started another war. The Americans ended up with half of these disputed islands.

An early colorful character once owned Drake's third landing site. Find out what he and Drake had in common. See how Drake's Nova Albion has grown and what this country is like today. Follow his route from bay to bay and imagine where he hid Spanish treasure that may contain a falcon of gold and emeralds as long as a man's finger. Discover a lost part of history.

Fourteen years as a sport and commercial salmon fisherman in the area of where Drake landed have given me the insight as to how the tides run, the direction of the winds, and where landmarks are located. Many of the important landmarks are only visible from the water.

As a gill-netter who fished at night drifting with the tides, when possible, I kept visual contact with these landmarks. Years later, with pictures taken of an old rock carving located on a prominent point that jets out into the bay and while doing research on the Spanish names in the area, is when this historical event came to light.

The natives in this country are the Coast Salish, who have fished their territory for centuries and still do today. Unknown to Drake on route through Nova Albion, he made contact with at least four different tribes, with different names and protected territories.

This long journey back in history encountered a lot of dead ends, including problems reading the old English language that contained many misspelled words, one of which has misdirected historians big time. But as a whole, a fascinating trip that seemed to flow in slow motion compared to the fast track of today. In solving the Drake landing mystery, the information came one small piece at a time, always with another question and a big surprise, until an entirely new picture developed from what has been recorded. The main question that prevailed through all the research and what made this so interesting is, did Drake really leave a treasure behind in Nova Albion?

Everything points to" "yes, he did," and the John Drake chapter leads to that conclusion. Without a doubt, treasure hunters will want to know Drake's 20-mile line of travel through his new country. And for those who have studied Drake's famous voyage, be ready for surprises.

H. R. Wagner, a foremost authority on Francis Drake, in *Spanish Explorations in the Strait of Juan de Fuca*, almost solved the Drake landing mystery. He looked right at the bay he had spent years searching for and didn't make the connection. One point here is, sometimes the lack of information can be just as important as what is written. In this case, three different histories, English, Spanish, and American, all waver in the same location.

Mrs. Zelia Nuttall, in *New Light on Drake*, supplied important English documents with the names of some of Drake's crew. One unusual name is carved in stone at Drake's monument. She also determined that Drake left crew behind in Nova Albion. See where these castaways ended up.

Both Mrs. Nuttall and Mr. Wagner provided important information that helped construct the missing pieces of Drake's famous voyage, and all their extensive research helped solve the lost North American landing of Sir Francis Drake.

Because this history covers such a long timeline, only important events and their associated histories that connect to Drake's North American landing are covered here. Besides the old Portus Map, the next clue to this mystery happened in the harbor of Veracruz while on a slave trading venture to the New World.

Harry S. Truman, 33rd President of the United States, once said, *"the only thing new in this world is history you don't know."*

1

The Battle
of San Juan de Ulúa

A bugle sounded. Smoke billowed from the decks as cannonballs whistled into the ship's planking. Hidden soldiers with bayonets fixed streamed out of the fortress of San Juan de Ulúa while others jumped on board docked English ships. The surprise attack lasted six hours, a bloodbath for the outnumbered Englishmen. During the battle, three English ships sank—one while still tied to the dock—but not without a fight. English gunners zeroed in on three Spanish ships, two of which first listed and then headed for the bottom. The third burned to the waterline.

In 1568, out of a fleet of five English ships, headed by John Hawkins, that had landed in the Spanish seaport, only two ships escaped the harbor of Veracruz. First to escape was the 50-ton *Judith,* commanded by Francis Drake, followed by the 350-ton *Minion* commanded by John Hawkins, loaded with survivors of the battle. Before the fleet had left England, the Spanish had sailed warships into Plymouth harbor as a warning for Hawkins to stay out of the Caribbean. And he did so, but on the voyage back north to catch the easterly winds to England, extreme storm damage in the Gulf of Mexico forced the fleet into the only harbor available. Bad timing for the English: The day after docking, the Spanish merchant fleet showed up with 13 ships, escorted by two warships, for their annual visit. And on board, the new Viceroy of New Spain, Don Martin Enriquez de Almansa, who after docking next to the English ships planned and ordered the attack. His actions were responsible for the slaughter of 500 Englishmen. Captured seamen were hung, burned at the stake, or employed as slaves.

How It Began

The Spanish attack in the harbor of Veracruz reflected more than the English trespassing. A deep religious hate existed. In the early 1500's Roman Catholics controlled England, but the teachings of a German cleric, Martin Luther, began to spread throughout western European countries. When the Catholic Church denied King Henry VIII permission to divorce his first wife, Spanish Princess Catherine of Aragon, Henry took control of the Church of England and did away with Roman Catholic influence. Under the Act of Six Articles, England became a Catholic Orthodoxy. The Orthodox Church was evangelical, but not Protestant; it was Catholic, but not Roman. So both Roman Catholics and Protestants in England met persecution, known as "the bloody whip with six strings."

By modifying England's religion, all the tax money that flowed to Rome ended up in Henry's coffers. His plan worked. Plus, he confiscated Catholic land holdings, the monasteries, and sold them to the highest bidder. But one unforeseen consequence of Henry's actions resulted in a generational change. At the time over half of his subjects were young, under 18, including some who would become nobles and advisers. They enjoyed the split from Rome and the newfound freedoms in the Protestant religion that took a strong foothold in England.

In 1541, King Henry proclaimed himself King of Ireland, another Roman Catholic country. This he achieved by paying the Irish nobles to accept his rule. But in the latter part of his reign the money ran out, which caused unrest and strife in Ireland. At the end of Henry's reign, England was broke and deep in debt.

Proceeding down the monarchy of England, the Tudors, came Edward VI, King Henry's only son. Henry's two older daughters, Mary and Elizabeth, were both banished from the monarchy until Katherine Parr, Henry's sixth wife, reintroduced them to their father. She, through her calm and collective way, assisted them back into the line of succession, but behind young Edward. So Edward, at the age of nine, became king. Guided by counsel, he did away with King Henry's Six Articles and presented a new prayer book that omitted Latin and that led to England becoming a Protestant country.

At the same time, young Edward continued his father's Reformation in Ireland, a bad decision for a country in turmoil. So in 1548, England appointed Sir Edward Bellingham as Lord Deputy of Ireland. His challenge dealt with reforms imposed on the Irish by King Henry VIII. Furthermore, he addressed the problem of Roman Catholic influence supported and funded by Spain, which at the time was the most powerful country in the world.

After the unforeseen death of young Edward VI at the age of 16 came Mary I, "Bloody Mary," King Henry's firstborn. She attempted to change England's religion back to Catholic and burned over 300 Protestants at the stake. She also confiscated Irish land to give to English settlers. In addition, she married Prince Phillip of Spain, although he abandoned her to claim the Spanish throne. With the death of Mary, whose reign only lasted five years, Phillip II of Spain claimed the thrown of England, but that never happened. Elizabeth, Mary's younger sister, became Queen. She broke a promise to her older sister on her deathbed to retain the Roman Catholic religion and proclaimed England a Protestant country.

Elizabeth I, the Virgin Queen, allowed private enterprises to flourish, breaking trade embargoes and disrupting Catholic shipping to the New World. Spanish, Portuguese, and even French ships became targets of the English privateers (private-men-of-war). Not only did Catholic ships lose cargo, often times their ships became part of the booty.

The Spanish called Francis Drake a *Corsair*, others called him a thief. His countrymen used the more dignified name, privateer. But whatever his title should be, Drake earned the reputation as the most feared and hated enemy of Spain and the Roman Catholic world.

After the unprovoked attack at San Juan de Ulúa, which Spain touted as a great victory, Drake vowed to recover damages. He would never return to the slave trade with his cousin John Hawkins, but instead sailed for the Caribbean in 1570 with the *Dragon* and *Swan*. He went there again in 1571, but with only the *Swan*, to gain intelligence. While there he established a base his crew called "Port Plenty," a hidden harbor located in eastern Panama. Drake buried needed supplies for his operations at this hot and humid harbor surrounded by jungle. Early Spanish attempts to settle the area failed. The sweltering climate made the whole area a miserable place to live.

From his early voyages to the Caribbean, Drake developed a grand plan to attack the Spanish silver train. According to *Sir Francis Drake Revived*, a raiding party with the help of escaped Spanish slaves, called cimaroons, traveled overland through the jungle to intercept mules packing gold, silver, and jewels from Panama to Nombra de Dios. But they were discovered and had to fight their way back to their boats. During the conflict they still found Spain's treasure house. They discovered silver bars that weighed 35 to 40 pounds each. The Spaniards had the bars stacked 12 feet high, 10 feet wide, and 17 feet long. This first view of Spanish riches overwhelmed the Englishmen, but the predicament they found themselves in forced them to leave it all behind.

Later, on a second attempt and with the help of a French privateer, Captain Tetû (Guillaume Le Testu), they did intercept the silver train. The raiding party stole more booty than they could handle, so they buried the excess. The Spanish, however, found the cache and retrieved part of their treasure. This profitable venture made Drake a rich commoner, but it came at a high cost. He took a Spanish shot in the leg and almost bled to death. He would carry the Spanish ball for the rest of his life and had to drag his leg when he walked. His brother John took a Spanish shot and died when he attempted to board an armed frigate, and his brother Joseph died, along with others, after they caught the fever, possibly from drinking bad water. French Captain Tetû fell behind the escaping Englishmen and was captured and killed by the Spaniards, who then displayed his head in the marketplace.

Before the second raid on the silver train, French Captain Tetû, an older man and a scholar, brought news of his country. He told a story of a massacre at Saint Bartholomew in 1572, where Catholic mob violence killed thousands of Huguenots, French Protestants. This story by the French Captain is an important piece to the larger puzzle of Drake's lost landing. H. R. Wagner, an authority on Francis Drake, missed how this name fit in and found the name insignificant. What confused Wagner is that while on his famous voyage, Drake named an island in the Strait of Magellan "Bartholomew". This name is important, because it will later answer a "why" question. Francis Fletcher, the pastor on Drake's famous voyage, would declare August 24th as St. Bartholomew's Day. He would preach about this incident in France, where he held two services a day.

Furthermore, "Bartholomew" will also show up on a statement made to Spanish interrogators by Drake's young cousin John, captured in 1582, after he deserted the Fenton Expedition. John, as a page and artist, helped document Drake's famous voyage around the world.

After disrupting Spanish shipping in the Caribbean and raiding the silver train, Drake knew greater riches could be obtained in the Pacific trade. Escaped Spanish slaves, cimaroons, led him to a high lookout in western Panama where he could observe this vast new sea. This sparked Drake's need to sail in that ocean. So in 1577, he executed a plan that would enhance England's financial standing, by paying off her debts. To get permission from the crown for any voyage meant that his country took a share of the proceeds. So with papers and permission, his grand plan was to follow the same route taken around the bottom of South America by the fleet of Ferdinand Magellan, first to sail around the world.

Only Drake and his private backers knew the destination of this top-secret venture. Recruiters told the crew that their heading was Alexandria. The real objective is not known, but some believe he planned to explore the spice trade. Others claim he was on a secret mission for the Queen. Whatever the aim, his famous voyage would send a shock wave all the way to Spain—complaints were filed with the English Government even before he made his way home in 1580.

Before the start of the 1577 voyage, Drake outfitted the *Elizabeth*, the *Benedict*, the *Marigold*, the *Swan*, and his flagship, the *Pelican*, in different locations. Three ships he outfitted in Ireland so as not to draw attention or give a hint that he was putting a fleet together. Catholic spies observed all naval activity, and if Spain caught wind of an English fleet heading out into the Atlantic, Drake would lose his best weapon, surprise.

English privateers used small ships, converted merchant ships, out-fitted for war. Although Drake's flagship the *Pelican* was not English, she was a 100-ton French ship, redesigned and strengthened with a double-sheeted hull. These ships sailed fast and steered well, whereas Spanish ships displayed a bulky design, with poor steering, and they sailed slow.

The total crew count between the five ships numbered about 140 to 164. They consisted of soldiers, a barrel maker, a druggist, a shoe-maker, a tailor, and even musicians along with gentlemen and boys. On the famous voyage, Drake took three relatives, his teenage cousin John, another cousin William Hawkins, and his younger brother Thomas.

The head of the fleet, Francis Drake, stood about five feet four inches tall, an average selected height for English seamen. Soldiers recruited stood taller so they could shoot over the top of seamen. Drake had thick hips and a round face with a light complexion. He wore a mustache along with a reddish goatee. He never trained in the English Navy, but he excelled in seamanship. How he learned these skills comes from two different accounts. The first says that as boys, Drake and two other brothers, John and Joseph, served as apprentice seamen in the William Hawkins family. The English frequently sent older children to more prosperous relatives for training and service. So under William Hawkins, a seafaring trader who sailed to European ports, including Spain, young Francis went to sea as a boy with other cousins. The most noted of his cousins, John Hawkins, was a headstrong SOB well trained by his father. His calling sought riches in the African slave trade, and on his good side, he excelled in ship design.

While in training, young Francis grew up observing the Devon coast society. These prosperous seafaring traders made their living importing and exporting goods, some of which they gained through piracy. Their wealth started to grow under the reign of King Henry VIII, when he expanded and updated shipbuilding in England, renewing the English privateer in the style of the famous Harry Paye from Poole. These ventures enlisted private armies, all funded and under the direction of rich upper-class families. The ships that William Hawkins commandeered hailed from Catholic countries and were dealing in illegal contraband, as he often did. But authorities caught the elder Hawkins after he looted a Spanish ship during the five-year reign of Queen Mary and he spent time in prison. So while under the thumb of the Hawkins family, young Francis learned the basics for his controversial career.

The opposing account of Drake growing up and learning seamanship is that he worked for an older man on a coastal trading vessel, who upon his death willed Francis his ship. Drake then sold the ship and invested the money in a Hawkins trading venture. This story doesn't add up. First, ships in those years had a short life, about ten years before woodworms burrowed through the planking. By the time Francis would have learned his trade and received the ship, the vessel would have been worthless. If

Drake did sell a ship, one can guess that it came from one of the Hawkins trading ventures and had been commandeered from a Catholic country. For Drake to know what he did about navigation and a strategy for intercepting ships, he needed first-hand experience. Furthermore, he became a skilled archer, an accomplishment worthless to protect a small coastal trading vessel. So his connection to the Hawkins family fits with his career choice. Plus, he would later follow the service and training practice when he took his young uneducated cousin John under his wing.

Between his connection with Hawkins and home, Francis learned to read and write when most of his fellows received no education at all. His father Edmond, once a sailor, then a farmer, became a Protestant preacher. Because of Catholic mob violence, the family fled to Kent, where they took up residence in the hull of a ship. Like his father, young Francis learned scriptures and became effective in dealing with people, something he already had a head start on, because he grew up with 11 brothers. The English kept no birth records for commoners, so some writers claim he was firstborn, while others claim he was second.

While Francis was affiliated with Hawkins, they had no preference in religion and attended both churches. The Spanish actually thought that John Hawkins was Catholic. But as always, during service and training young minds pick up behaviors that are not beneficial. So while in training under Hawkins, Francis picked up things you don't learn as a preacher's son. He liked to brag and always had the grand plan, acted the big shot, and enjoyed attention. But when challenged, he could revert to scriptures. Like a preacher, he used salesmanship to gain rich backers for his famous voyage. One investor, Sir Francis Walsingham, spymaster for Elizabeth I, helped promote Drake's career. And if one were to guess, he controlled the cover-up of Drake's 1577 voyage.

Young Francis gained experience sailing to the Azores under Hawkins and later battled the North Sea transporting soldiers and cargo to Ireland, where he witnessed the carnage of war. In 1577, he was about 30 years old. He didn't know his birth day. Historians put his birth around 1540 to 1542, about six or seven years younger than Elizabeth I. At the start of his famous voyage he had already spent three-quarters of his life at sea and had earned the full respect of his crew. On shore he displayed a jubilant personality, but when he put on his scarlet cap with a gold band, the crew knew who was in charge. They called him general, a title usually associated with the army.

One characteristic that stands out about Drake is that he was an achiever, a self-starter. He pushed himself and his crew. This came to light on the first attempt to raid the Spanish silver train when his men became discouraged and wanted to call off the raid and head back to the boats. Drake gave them a pep talk. He stated that they only had one chance to complete what they came for or go home and live in poverty. Then he passed out from the wound in his leg. So he possessed an inner drive to break with the poverty of his past under a two-class English system.

Portraits of Drake from his later years are an important piece of the puzzle for his lost landing. In them, he projects his power, authority, and accomplishments by pointing his index finger next to the world globe. If he had anything to say about the composition of his portraits, then his pointing index finger is shown. This symbol to him meant something special, possibly learned from his father's preaching or from his early years as an apprentice seaman, by being directed to do the dirtiest jobs. Another possible source may have come from the books of the time. These to him were powerful, and when the cover was opened, they showed a hand with a pointing index finger. Drake's symbol of using a pointing index finger is documented in the *Anonymous Narrative*. This sign of authority helped solve his North American landing mystery.

In England, his fellow countrymen were split about his actions against Spain. The common Englishman viewed him as a hero, whereas English Catholics loathed him and were ready to report any information directly to their Spanish connections. Later, Spain would put a hefty reward on his head, and a plot to kill him was foiled. The British Admiralty never accepted him either and only called on his services as a last resort. He lacked the birthright and discipline required by the English Navy. He did listen to others' point of view, but never followed orders and did everything his way. There is no doubt that later decisions he made to attack the Spanish Port of Cadiz in a forthcoming 1588 war with Spain did benefit his country and hinder the Spanish war effort.

To become a sea captain Drake paid his dues the hard way, from the bottom up. With superb navigation skills and his connection with ship designer John Hawkins, private backers supplied the latest weapons and sailing technology of the time. But all the best equipment and knowhow are sometimes not enough. Drake, his captains, and his crew all knew the dangers of heading to sea and facing the elements. On his famous voyage, he would push his luck and face extreme peril when he directed his ships into uncharted waters.

Start of the Famous Voyage

Once Drake's fleet met up at sea in 1577 and headed south in the Atlantic, storm damage forced them back to Plymouth. After this bad start, the fleet started out once again in early December. Along their route, the West African coast, they stopped and traded for fresh food. While there, they assembled a prefab boat called a pinnace that had been stored in the *Pelican*'s cargo hold. With the speedy little craft they chased down Spanish fishing vessels. Heading farther south they captured two Portuguese caravels. So early on Catholic ships suffered the loss of their catch and whatever commodities they carried. Continuing south, Drake decided one of the captured Portuguese ships was better than the *Benedict*, so he exchanged ships and named the 40-ton fishing vessel *Christopher.*

Off the Cape Verde Islands they captured another Portuguese ship, the best prize so far, loaded with wine, along with canvas and cloth. The crew relished their wine and any other spirits they could get their hands on. While at sea they received only one meal a day and the wine helped filled that empty spot. Plus the drink helped kill the monotony of a long sea voyage.

The captured Portuguese ship made frequent trips to Brazil, and that was its destination. So Drake seized her charts and added the ship to his fleet. After he renamed the ship *Mary,* he assigned Thomas Doughty responsibility for the soldiers on the ship. On board was Nuña da Silva, the owner and navigator, an older man in his late fifties with a dark complexion. He displayed a long graying beard and most of the time wore a body-length black coat. Drake needed his knowledge. No English ships had ventured where they were heading and any maps Drake may have acquired of the route were without detail. So any good luck Silva may have possessed ran out. Drake would carry this navigator all the way to lower Mexico. And even after his release, the poor man would face Spanish interrogators who tortured anyone who had helped Drake.

Now below the equator and able to view the Southern Cross in the night sky, the fleet caught the westerly wind flow and crossed the Atlantic. Off the Brazilian coast, they turned south using Silva's charts to avoid Portuguese ports. Along the coast, the ships anchored numerous times. Always short on food, they experienced either feast or famine. They lived off birds, seals, and fish, and in some cases discovered fresh fruit. The fleet encountered pounding storms, and three ships disappeared only to show up again, relieving everyone's concerns. When Silva's ship, the *Mary*, fell behind, that caused an extreme concern, because she contained the wine. After the *Christopher*, taken from the Portuguese, disappeared and reappeared a second time, Drake transferred all the cargo off and set the ship adrift. Then at Port Desire they cut up the *Swan*, a fly-boat, for firewood. Now with a smaller fleet that could stay together, they headed south toward Port San Julian at the bottom of South America.

Although Drake controlled his crew, along the way trouble broke out. Thomas Doughty, in charge of the soldiers and assigned to Silva's ship, the *Mary*, evidently took valuable items considered part of the common booty. This theft resulted in accusations and arguments. Drake intervened by taking over the *Mary* and transferring Doughty to his flagship. Doughty now thought he commanded the *Pelican*, and that created more trouble. The crew, the captains, and even the gentlemen started picking sides, and tensions built. By the time the fleet landed at Port San Julian, Drake had opposition to his command. Was that Doughty's plan all along, to disrupt and hinder the voyage? This question will never be answered, but Doughty came from an old Catholic family and must have known or thought Drake had ill intentions planned against Catholic holdings in the Pacific. Whether he took it upon himself or received orders from a higher source to sabotage the voyage, only he knew.

While in Port San Julian, Drake, his officers, and the gentlemen met on the *Pelican* and ordered a trial, where they convicted Doughty of mutiny. An execution took place in accordance with English law, and Doughty lost his head while his brother hopelessly stood by and would never be the same. Silva would later claim that Doughty planned to run off with the ships.

At the same time, Drake took care of another grievance that could possibly create more tension on the voyage. Complaints surfaced among the crew that the gentlemen, always demanding, did nothing to pull their own weight. So Drake settled the affair before more trouble broke out. He issued orders that everyone would work, even the gentlemen.

Port San Julian is a desolate place with food scarce and the weather cold. To keep warm they broke up Silva's ship, the *Mary*, for firewood. On shore they observed a famous landmark: a gallows with bones on the ground left by Magellan, the Portuguese captain working for Spain in 1520. He also had experienced mutiny and had taken the appropriate action. The cooper spotted good wood in the gallows, so he took the structure down and made a water barrel. But no one on board would drink out of it.

The native inhabitants towered above the shorter Englishmen. In one encounter, one of the Englishmen attempted to show the natives that he could shoot his own bow and arrow, not at them, but his string broke, and the natives perceived his actions as a threat. They killed two of Drake's crew with arrows in the chest. One of the soldiers shot back and hit one of them in the belly, and after that the natives stayed clear of the Englishmen. Although the Englishmen never went far from their ships, in the distance they could see the glow of native fires. With a favorable wind, on August 17th the *Pelican*, the *Marigold*, and the *Elizabeth* departed the barren port and headed out to the west.

In 1578, after battling terrific storms, mutiny, and extreme hardship, Drake directed his ships toward the Strait of Magellan. This strait cuts through the southern tip of South America, at that time the only known route to the Pacific. But the winds turned contrary, so they anchored at the entrance to wait. Here, according to H. R. Wagner, Drake renamed his ship as the *Golden Hind*. This name comes from the symbol atop the coat of arms of one of the fleet's investors, Sir Christopher Hatton. This event never took place. Captains never renamed their ship during a voyage—to do so would mean bad luck—so whoever added the entry in the footnotes of *The Famous Voyage* was not a sea captain and didn't know the implications. Drake may have come across as a religious figure, but as a seaman he would follow the age-old superstitions so as not to freak out his crew. Furthermore, not everyone in England followed the religious teaching of the time; some towns and hamlets where Drake drew his sailors and soldiers from stilled lived in the Dark Ages and believed in witchcraft. But captured ships were a different story. Drake renamed the ships he kept. The renaming of his ship before entering the Strait of Magellan is a part of an English cover-up that will come to light later. Drake did return to England with a ship named the *Golden Hind*, but the naming event will happen later in the new country he named Nova Albion. That is where his dreams of grandeur will kick in.

The winds changed and the fleet maneuvered the narrows of the Strait of Magellan on August 24th, St. Bartholomew's Day. Here they spotted three islands, two of which showed native inhabitants, so they anchored next to the southernmost island away from the locals. These three islands Drake named, Elizabeth, Saint Bartholomew, and Saint George. While there, according to Pastor Francis Fletcher, the crew butchered two thousand penguins without making a dent in their numbers. He also stated that the meat tasted good and not fishy. But more important, everyone filled their bellies.

Under way again on the 26th, the winds changed and changed again, not in their favor. The ships would anchor, try again, and anchor again. On one of the many stops they met the local natives who fished and camped on the islands, the Alaculoofs, in a boat made of bark. Pastor Fletcher reported that the men painted their faces with red circles around their eyes and red stripes on their forehead that set off their long dark hair. They dressed in skins that hung to their elbows and knees and carried crud tools, sharp hatches and knives made from mussel shells. The women wore strings of white shells around their neck, and the same decorated their arms. These females, as in all extremely cold climates, were pleasingly plump. But more impressive was their bark boat—the bow looked like the stern and held the whole family. Never in all their travels had they seen a craft that compared.

Turning the bend in the Strait of Magellan, they got their first view of the high snow-capped mountains on both sides of the strait. On shore, they investigated an evergreen tree whose bark smelled and tasted like cinnamon. John Winter, the captain of the *Elizabeth,* peeled the bark and

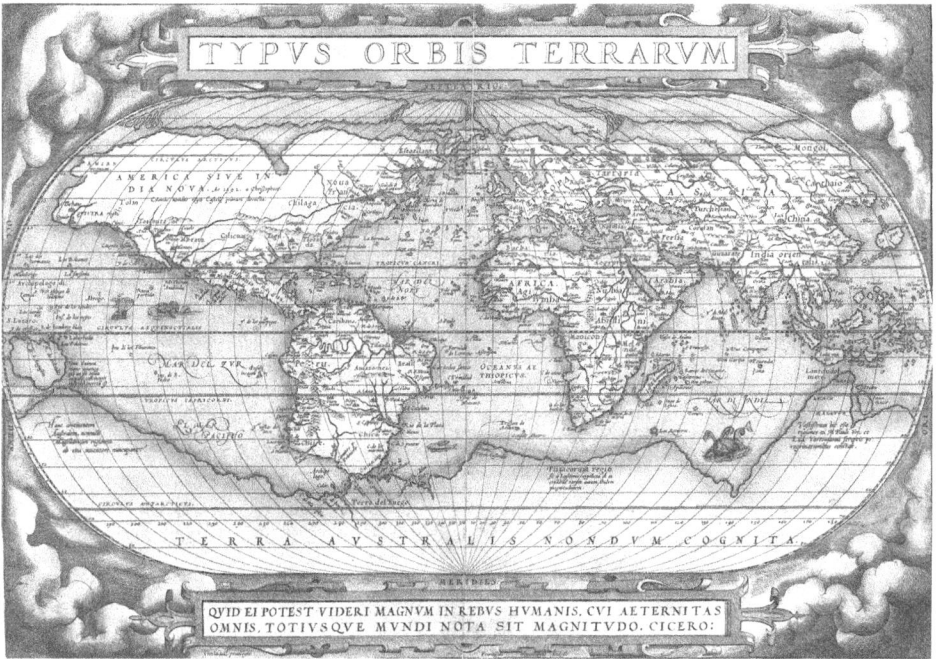

Abraham Ortelius World Map, Typvs Orbis Terrarvm, 1570.

stored it for the long voyage home. This is a clue to the fleet's true mission, the intent to explore the spice trade in the Moluccas or Spice Islands.

At the north end of the strait, the mountains closed in and the passage came to what looked like a dead end. Drake sent a launch looking for a way through. First, they explored back south into Whale Sound and found no channel there. Then he sent a launch north, where they did find a narrow channel, but only one-half a league wide, with no room for mistakes. If the wind changed while in what is now known as Crooked Reach and Long Reach, the ships could have real problems. So once the launch returned, with no other options and the conditions right, the fleet hauled anchor and started through the passage. Luck prevailed and the fleet sailed into the South Pacific.

With a good wind on the stern and the help of the Humboldt or Peru current that streams toward the equator, the fleet headed out into the Pacific. According to Wagner, Drake relied on the Ortelius map, which looks nothing like later maps. It showed the lower Chilean coast with a big bulge that protruded west and Terra Australis as a continent across the entire southern Pacific.

Once out in the Pacific, they set a northwest course, but something appeared wrong with the Ortelius map. No land showed up off the ship's bow. The big bulge did not exist. So they kept the high snow-capped mountains to the east in view and continued on to the northwest. This heading would take them to the westerly trade winds and the Spice Islands or China or both. Nothing written indicates that the fleet intended to attack any Spanish ports. Plus, they didn't know the location of any ports. Spain kept all their charts of the Pacific secret from all other countries.

The Ortelius map displayed the Pacific as only a thousand miles wide, one-third the real distance, and on the northern section of the map, it showed the narrow passageway of Anian, a route back to the Atlantic. If the fleet encountered any Spanish ships along their planned course, they would be fair game. But, the fleet's original plans went up in smoke when the wind began to blow.

While on course to the northwest the winds changed, light at first, but contrary. The ships started to tack, then about a week and a half into the voyage the winds gained force and turned into a full-blown gale. The captains ordered the sails down and everything lashed to the deck. They experienced a pounding ride and used a sea anchor to keep the bow into the waves as the wind drove them back south. During the gale, on September 28th, the *Marigold,* a 30-ton bark, disappeared. As the storm subsided, Drake could only see the 80-ton *Elizabeth,* but the captains carried a plan for the ships getting separated. They would meet off the Chilean coast at 30° latitude. John Thomas, the *Marigold's* captain, was important to Drake. He spoke fluent Spanish and on his travels had once been to China. Drake's recruitment of Thomas is another clue that speaks to where the fleet planned to explore. What Drake didn't know at the time is that the *Marigold* foundered in the storm, and when the ship went down her crew never had a chance in the icy cold sea. All hands were lost.

The powerful gale blew the other two ships so far south they ended up back where they had entered the Pacific. Desperately in need of water, Drake attempted to send a launch ashore but abandoned the effort when the winds picked up again. Only this time, John Winter, captain of the *Elizabeth,* deserted. He headed back into the Strait of Magellan and then back for England. With a haze and giant waves between the ships, Drake didn't see his ship depart. Captain Winter was no friend of Drake. He supported Doughty in his mutinous actions and would use any excuse to abandon the voyage. And when he did so, he took half of the fighting force with him. Later, back in England when Drake returned, authorities arrested Captain Winter for desertion. The court sentenced him to hang and were about to carry out the judgment when Drake stepped in and blocked his execution.

As the storm raged for a second time, the wind blew the *Pelican* so far south from the Strait of Magellan that Drake discovered another route around the bottom of South America. He then knew that the continent of Terra Australis did not exist and he could not depend on the Ortelius Map. Instead, he discovered a series of islands, one of which he landed on and chiseled the name of the Queen, along with the date, on a large rock. There is a dispute over how far south the storm blew the *Pelican.* Some say 57°, others say 55°, but what is clear is that Drake found another route around the bottom of South America. Later, in 1582, navigators he sent with the Fenton Expedition planned to use his discovery to bypass and elude any Spanish forces guarding the Strait of Magellan. Spain had never journeyed or explored that far south in the Pacific and didn't know another route around the bottom of South America existed.

The winds changed and with the storm over, the *Pelican* headed back north toward the Chilean coast to search for the separated ships. Summer arrived in the lower hemisphere and on this course they sailed for the whole month of November. When they spotted an island, they stopped to search for water, collect firewood, and procure any food. They lived off birds and seals. Some of the lower islands had native inhabitants, the Yahgans, who also made bark boats, but of a different construction than the Alaculoofs in the Strait of Magellan. The natives they encountered in the lower Pacific were friendly and had never encountered any Spaniards. But as the *Pelican* sailed north toward 38°, off the Chilean coast, Drake would discover the hard way the impact of Spanish contact with local natives.

2

Into Spanish Colonial Territory

About 20 miles off the Chilean coast, within 38°, the lookout spotted a small island named Mocha. A landing party including Drake went ashore, where they traded with local natives for a couple of sheep and some corn. The next morning the same party of 12 returned to fill the water barrels and all hell broke loose. The natives were waiting in ambush. They immediately grabbed and killed Thomas Brewer and Thomas Flood heading for the water hole. At the same time, the warriors attacked the launch. Arrows and stones flew at the stunned mariners, while natives plunged into the water grabbing at the oars. The crew fought for their lives. They held up shields and swung blindly with swords. Quick thinking, one of the Englishmen reached over and cut the bow line that held the launch to shore. The battle ended when the water got too deep for the natives to follow, as the launch drifted out of harm's way. Everyone in the launch had a wound, some worse than others. Besides the loss of Brewer and Flood, Nele the master gunner would later die of his injuries. Two arrows struck Drake, one in the head and the other under his right eye.

Why the natives attacked the English goes back to 1551, when the Spanish first arrived and tried to take over their territory. The natives fought back and deterred the invaders. The Spanish called the area Tierra de Guerra, "land of war." Spain built settlements along the coast but could never secure this seven-mile-long island of Mocha. And the Englishmen, unaware, landed in the middle of a hornet's nest.

After the wounded party struggled back to the *Pelican*, Drake ordered full sails later that afternoon. They headed east toward the Chilean coast, which they followed with a good southerly wind until December 3rd. Short on food, the *Pelican* found and anchored in the bay of Quintero.

With no maps and a haze along the shore, the Englishmen didn't know they'd bypassed the Port of Santiago about 15 miles back. While at anchor, they met and entertained one of the local natives, who directed them to another native, known as Felipe, who spoke Spanish. Felipe informed Drake that he had bypassed a harbor where a large ship lay at anchor. So with Felipe as a guide, the *Pelican* headed back south and arrived at the port on December 5th.

When the *Pelican* pulled into the harbor of Valparaiso, Port of Santiago, the Spanish didn't recognize Drake's weather-beaten ship as English. And of course, the *Pelican* displayed no colors. The *Pelican* entered the harbor about noon far enough away from the anchored ship so the Spaniards couldn't see the cannon ports in the gunnels. Then a raiding party set out in the launch toward the unsuspecting ship. Drake's troops, besides being trained for war, were also hunger driven, and the Spaniards had no idea what was about to happen.

As the launch reached the ship, the Spaniards beat their drum and set out a cask of wine to welcome their fellow countrymen. Then terror struck. Soldiers swarmed on deck led by Tom Moon, who swung and hit the Spanish pilot in the face saying, "go down dog." One frightened Spaniard leaped overboard and hit the water paddling for shore. To secure the ship, the raiding party rounded up all the Spanish crew and herded them below deck. But the Spaniard who swam ashore proceeded to warn the town.

Drake immediately assembled more soldiers and headed for the settlement, but after the warning everyone had fled. The small town contained about eight houses and a church that the Englishmen tore apart. They pilfered all the food and any items of value. They even packed away the church bell, which in those years, the Spanish cast in silver. In the church they made off with ornaments that they gave to Pastor Fletcher, a kind gesture, but a joke. Fletcher didn't need such trinkets and disposed of them. Anything of real value Drake kept. A gold crucifix set with emeralds is one stolen item; whether it came from the church or the Spanish ship is not known.

The Spanish ship the soldiers stormed had a name, the *Los Reyes*, nicknamed the *Grand Capitana*, a square rigger claimed by the Spanish to be 200 tons, about 25 feet wide and 100 feet long, whereas Drake's flagship the *Pelican* had a rating of 100 tons, 20 feet wide and 75 feet long. The fully outfitted *Grand Capitana* destined for Peru had an interesting history that will come into play later on.

In November of 1567, the *Los Reyes* set sail from Callao, Port of Lima, to follow up on an old Inca story about gold and riches in a land to the west. Well, of course, the Incas only wanted to get rid of the Spanish. But a Spanish soldier, Pedro Sarmiento de Gamboa, bought into the old story and received permission from the Governor General, Lope Garcia de Castro, to make the voyage. But instead of putting Sarmiento in command of the voyage, the Governor General put his young, inexperienced nephew, Álvaro de Mendaña de Neira, in charge. Mendaña didn't care about the old Inca stories of gold. He wanted to convert any natives, or as he put it, "heathens to Christianity." Sarmiento disliked the Governor General's decision, but accepted it just to make the voyage. So when the *Los Reyes* and a second ship, called the *Todos Santos*, reached Santa Isabel Island, one of the Solomon Islands, they discovered more than they had counted on, and it wasn't gold or riches.

The natives of the Solomon's tolerated the expedition's arrival, but they brought too many mouths to feed, 150 between the two ships, very trying on the Islanders' food supply. The Spaniards kept demanding more pork that the natives raised, but the swine were paramount to the native's economy, and tensions started to build between the two different cultures. So, the Islanders served an alternative meal that horrified the Spaniards: a quarter of a young boy with the arm and hand still attached. The Islanders were insulted when the Spanish refused to eat what they had presented. The stunned Spaniards left Santa Isabel Island and charted the remaining Solomon group, then headed back to Peru. But before they reached home many on the expedition died of scurvy.

Pedro Sarmiento, second in command of the *Los Reyes* on the Solomon expedition, under Álvaro de Mendaña, would later write about his experiences. Plus, he would write about Drake's raid up the South American coast. H. R. Wagner used Sarmiento's account in his book, *Sir Francis Drake's Voyage Around the World*.

Back in Valparaiso, as part of the booty, Drake would keep this noted Spanish ship, the *Los Reyes*. On board as prisoners, according to Silva, were 15 or 16 Spaniards and Negroes. Silva also claimed the ship carried a load of timber, cut cedar boards. These boards would serve Drake's needs; cedar made a fast, hot fire for cooking, whereas beach wood they collected was damp, round, and bulky, plus full of sand. In the ship's hold, the Englishmen loaded 1770 jars of wine discovered in a warehouse, not counting the jars the raiding party sampled. When Drake searched the *Grand Capitana*, he discovered 4000 pesos in gold, according to the Spanish registry.

But that wasn't all: Hidden away under the steering he found a metal chest with more gold. Captains in the Spanish silver trade often did a little business under the table and did not register all their proceeds. Who better to know how the captains made a good living than Drake. That is why he combed the *Los Reyes* from end to end, as he would all other ships he would later commandeer. So how much unregistered booty did Drake find in captured Spanish ships? The captains surely weren't telling and the Spanish treasury didn't know. But, the big question here is, did Drake keep his own personal stash hidden away?

What brought this question to mind is Drake's history. When the Spanish attacked the English fleet at San Juan de Ulua, John Hawkins gave Drake orders to get out of the harbor and wait in the outer waters, but he didn't follow orders. He sailed for England with the fleet's treasure chest on board. Once home, he hid the proceeds before he spread the news of what happened in the Spanish port. After Hawkins escaped the harbor, he couldn't find Drake, and that forced him to set 100 crew members ashore to make it home on their own, which is another story of survival, torture, and death, not included here. When Hawkins arrived back in England, authorities arrested and jailed Drake. But he claimed he hid the treasure chest for safekeeping, and there wasn't any evidence to prove he had other intentions. So the crown released him. Part of the proceeds belonged to the Queen. She owned two of the ships on loan to Hawkins that were destroyed in the harbor of Veracruz. This incident shows Drake experienced a personality change when it came to gold or any other eye-catching riches. Thus the question, what part of the captured Spanish booty did Drake personally keep hidden away?

After the long and dangerous journey from home, this first taste of Spanish gold and riches taken with little conflict put new life into the Englishmen. This may not have been what Drake originally planned for the voyage, but as an achiever he knew how to take advantage of a great opportunity.

On the *Grand Capitana,* or the *Los Reyes,* Drake discovered a Greek pilot called Juan working for Spain. Drake transferred Juan to the *Pelican,* along with his Spanish charts. He now owned an extra ship along with her pilot to guide the way up the Chilean coast. On September 6th, both ships left the harbor of Valparaiso. On Sunday the 7th, they stopped back in the harbor of Quintero to drop off their native guide, Felipe, who Drake thanked and rewarded. Then both ships headed up the coast toward 30°, which Drake had designated as a rendezvous point for his two other ships if they became separated. Once at the meeting area, they waited around for five days. But his two other ships never showed up. So, with the Spanish charts and the Greek pilot, Drake headed northwest for La Herradura on the Chilean coast.

When they arrived, the ships anchored a short distance from the seaport of La Serena, an important town in Chile. In need of water, a landing party rowed for shore with barrels. Scanning the area they spotted some pigs and in a fast and squealing chase, heard for half a mile, they caught two large hogs and some wieners, a big mistake. You can't make that kind of noise in a peaceful settlement without being heard, and that is what happened. The farmer heard the commotion and sent a warning out to La Serena. News spread like wildfire that two strange ships were anchored at La Herradura and their crew were pilfering the area. In the meantime, Drake's landing party sent their swine harvest back to the *Pelican,* not knowing that a force of Spanish horsemen and natives on foot were racing their way. The Spaniards caught the landing party filling the water barrels. The attack began with the surprised crewmen, without their launch, heading for a large rock in shallow water away from the sword-flashing Spaniards. One of the crew, John Minivy, fell behind and as he ran, a spear struck him in the back. From the ship, Drake spotted the Spaniards' intent, but all he could do was send a launch back to rescue his crew from the rock. Through a hail of arrows and spears, everyone piled into the skiff and started rowing back to the ships, when they observed the Spaniards with Minivy's head impaled on a spear. After the attackers left with their prize and once the area appeared safe, Drake sent a burial party ashore to care for Minivy's body.

Hauling anchor and leaving La Herradura that same night, even with two pilots, Nuño da Silva and Juan the Greek, the ships nearly hit a reef near the Pajaros Islands off the Ciquimbo Peninsula. Heading farther up the coast, both ships anchored near the Pajaros Islets and added to their food supply. Although the Islets offered flocks of birds and available water, they didn't stay long. They left when horsemen were spotted following them along the coast from La Serena. So Drake ordered full canvas to the wind until they came within 27°, where they anchored in Medio Cove within Salada Bay. They would stay in this cove until January 19th to do maintenance on the *Pelican*.

Historians are not sure what maintenance Drake ordered done to his ship on this important stopover, since natives had been observed milling around on shore. Did the crew clean the *Pelican*'s bottom for faster sailing? The answer is yes, they did, because all other maintenance on a ship can be done while sailing. This is how he cleaned the ship's bottom without going on shore: Drake spent one day in Medio Cove to see how low the tides ebbed and whether the bay was clear of rocks. He knew how much water his ship drew and how close she needed to get to shore to be tilted on her side.

Normally the process of tilting (careening) takes two anchors, one over the starboard side to hold the ship in place and the other on shore with a line attached high up on the mast. Then as the tide drops, a crew on shore pull on the mast line a little at a time as other crew members in a launch maneuver back and forth along the hull, working from the top down to clean off barnacles and grass. Then they swabbed heavy grease over the cleaned planking to make the bottom slick. This process did one-half of the ship's bottom at a time. Then they turned the ship around and repeated the task. As for the second anchor line on shore, Drake had two ships and didn't need the second anchor on the beach. He used the anchored *Los Reyes*, a larger and heavier ship, for his second deadhead. He did the cleaning process backwards, an anchor over the port side and the mast line low down on the deck of his second anchored ship. That way, if the natives or any Spaniards threatened the *Pelican*, they would need to carry their boats to the tide line and paddle out into the bay. And to do so would be a big mistake—they would be sitting ducks.

While in the cove, the crew dumped six pipes of tar overboard to make room on the *Pelican* for part of the Chilean wine stored on the *Los Reyes*. From belowdecks the crew hoisted up artillery and sections for a prefab sailing craft, called a pinnace. This is the second and last prefab boat they would assemble on the voyage; the first they had disposed of before crossing the Atlantic. The parts for the pinnace went to the wide deck of the *Los Reyes* to be assembled and caulked. The artillery also went to the *Los Reyes* to protect the *Pelican* while they cleaned and greased her bottom. In this cove, Drake knew that Spanish riches lay ahead and that all the preparations—assembling the pinnace, cleaning the ship's bottom for faster sailing, and readying his weaponry—would give him the best chance against any Spanish force.

Drake knew that Spanish gold, silver, and jewels moved along the South American coast toward Panama. He had first seen the area from Middle America when cimaroons guided him to a high lookout where he could observe this vast new ocean. Only this time he could strike without having to travel through the humid jungle and fight the Spaniards to rejoin his boats. This time he would take command of the Spaniard's' private sea.

With the pinnace assembled and a muzzle-loading cannon mounted in the bow, Drake sent Juan the Greek and 15 crew members back south to fill the water barrels and to look for his two lost ships. But they didn't stay away long. They returned in two days without water or spotting the ships. So, on January 19th, the fleet of three set sail up the Chilean coast. Still in need of water, the pinnace ran close to the shore in search of a stream or a river. Along this course, they encountered native fishermen without incident, but the locals could not lead them to any water. So the crew drank wine. Then on February 4th, the fleet anchored at the mouth of the Pisagua River, where they spotted the small settlement of Tarapacá.

A landing party headed for shore that evening and while searching the houses, they found a man sleeping. In his possession were silver bars worth about 3000 pesos. The man had packed the silver down a steep mountain trail from the Potosi mine on his string of llamas. Cerro de Potosi is a huge mountain of rich silver ore, and at the time it was one of the major sources of Spanish silver. All the refining took place at the mine, along with the Spanish tax collector stamping each 35- to 40-pound bar. On average, each llama could pack about 70 pounds, two bars at most.

Drake took the man, his silver, and his llamas, plus a large quantity of llama jerky, called charqui. Finally, after a long search they replenished the ship's water supply, and no doubt that night the crew, who had been living off birds, consumed a tasty llama feast. But after interrogating his new prisoner, Drake had a taste for something else—more silver.

The next day, as they continued up the coast, the heavy mist along the desert shoreline cleared when the Humboldt Current moved offshore. With his captured Spanish charts, Drake entered the Port of Arica, a main shipping port for silver heading to Lima. In the port they boarded two small ships at anchor. The first carried 37 bars of silver and a chest with about 500 pesos in coins. The bars weighed about the same as in Tarapacá and were also packed down from the Potosi mine by llamas.

On one of the small ships, the Englishmen found 300 jars of wine, so they added the vessel to the fleet. While they searched the second small ship for booty, a misplaced lantern or torch sparked a fire that burned the vessel to the waterline.

One interesting point here is that later, a Spanish prisoner who Drake invited to look in the *Pelican*'s hold said it was full of vegetables. There is no account of where the vegetables came from. Arica, unlike the rest of the mountainous and desert coastline, did have good land where the Spanish grew vegetables. According to Wagner, a raiding party headed for shore, but when they spotted horsemen they called off the landing. So, were the vegetables on one of the small ships, or did the Englishmen land?

Off these two ships the soldiers detained three men, who were transferred to the *Pelican*. They were a Corsican who owned the ship with the silver, his black slave, and a Fleming named Nicolas Jorje, who will later add important information about Drake's ships.

Departing Arica, the fleet headed for Chule, Port of Arequipa, a short distance away. From the interrogation of the new prisoners Drake gained information of another ship in the area, so he sent the pinnace near the shore to search the inlets. The fleet, now with three ships and the pinnace, proceeded slowly up the coast—too slowly, because it took two days to reach the harbor of Chule when the trip should have only taken one day. The pinnace finally located the other ship anchored in the harbor of Chule, but it was too late. Earlier, the ship had carried a load of silver, but word had gone out from Arica to warn the neighboring port.

So when the pinnace arrived, the raiding party found the ship emptied of 500 silver bars. The ship's sideboards were still wet well above the waterline, showing that the residents had scrambled to save their silver. On shore, the townsmen stood taunting the Englishmen, and on the hillside llamas could be seen packing the silver away. The angry Englishmen boarded the ship and found nothing. The residents removed everything, even the food and water. So the Englishmen hauled anchor and hoisted the sails while the captain and his crew on shore watched their ship sail away. That would be the last they would ever see of their ship as she headed out to meet the rest of Drake's fleet.

At this point, Drake knew he needed to move faster up the coast to stay ahead of the Spanish warning system. Next on his hit list, Callao, Port of Lima, located farther north. From what he learned in the Caribbean, the fastest way to raid along the coast required only one ship and a pinnace. In his fleet, he had three extra ships that would only slow him down, plus too many ships would draw attention, whereas one ship with the pinnace skirting the starboard wouldn't draw a second glance. One or two ships in the Spanish shipping lanes were a regular occurrence, but not a fleet. So Drake changed the size of his flotilla.

From the ship taken at Arica, the crew unloaded 300 jars of wine; from the *Los Reyes*, they took out wine and some lumber. The third ship, taken at Chule, carried nothing. So off the coast of Arequipa, the crew raised the canvas on all three ships and on February 9th turned them loose to the currents and the wind. This left Drake with only the *Pelican* and the pinnace, the fastest way to sail and the best way to avoid detection.

From the *Pelican*, Drake let his prisoners watch as the three ships departed; they were Silva, Juan the Greek, and the Fleming Nicolas Jorje. What happened to other Spanish prisoners is unclear; if there were any, they were released aboard a fishing boat he stopped earlier off the coast of Arica. But Drake would keep all the black slaves who crossed his path, adding them to the crew.

Drake's earlier slave trading ventures to the New World under his cousin John Hawkins went against his grain. On his own, he did a complete turnaround and freed the people he once sold. The total count of blacks or maroons, as they were called, is unclear. There should have been four or five or more. One black, Diego, who originally started the famous voyage, is reported to have died of wounds suffered on the Island of Mocha, but Sir Richard Hawkins spotted him in England years later. Three maroons came from the *Los Reyes* and another from the small ship at the Port of Arica. And Drake would later free other blacks from their Spanish owners.

On the same day, February 9th, Drake intercepted another small ship, but turned her loose. She carried 200 jars of wine that he left on board. He didn't want to waste the time to unload her, plus they had enough wine for now. Other things occupied Drake's mind, like more silver. On course for Callao, Port of Lima, they spotted three small ships. Drake intercepted the one sailing farthest out from shore and questioned the captain, Gasper Martin. Martin gave up information about three ships loaded with silver. Two ships were in Callao and the third, of San Juan de Anton, had already left the port heading for Panama. 'Drake took three men off Martin's ship, one of them as a pilot to guide the *Pelican* into Callao. As they headed toward the major Spanish seaport, the *Pelican* had to pass through shallow water, but Drake didn't know that; he thought the pilot was about to run his ship aground, and he lost his temper and threatened to hang the pilot. But as it turned out, the *Pelican* sailed through without incident and reached Callao about ten o'clock that night.

Conflicting reports as to the number of ships anchored in the Port of Lima range from 7 to as many as 30. Somewhere in the middle seems reasonable, because Drake's men in the pinnace only searched the harbor for two hours. As a dark shadow the Englishmen went from ship to ship, ready to board any ship riding low in the water. But all the ships were empty. The silver hadn't been transported down to port yet. The Spaniards still had it stored in Lima. So Drake's crew disabled all the large ships by cutting their anchor lines, thinking they would drift out to sea. Instead they drifted on to shore.

In the meantime, the ship of Alonsó Rodriguez Bautista entered the port and dropped anchor. His ship carried merchandise bound for Lima. From shore, the harbormaster noticed the arrival of two new ships, so in the port's launch, he and his crew rowed out to inspect their cargo. He checked out Bautista's ship first and then started to board the *Pelican* when he immediately jumped back in his launch and started yelling, "Frenchmen, Frenchmen." He had spotted cannons and knew no Spanish trading vessels in the Pacific were armed. Drake's archers shot at the escaping harbormaster and hit his fast-moving launch but missed the ducking occupants. One Spaniard recognized an arrow that stuck in the launch as being English, so the alarm changed to "Englishmen."

As the harbormaster yelled out the warning, the raiding party in the pinnace reached Bautista's ship. They ordered her to strike sail, but Bautista refused and opened fire on the pinnace, killing one of Drake's crew. Bautista then ordered his men to cut the anchor line and they started back out to sea. Drake spotted the action and ordered his crew to haul the anchor. The *Pelican* then started out after Bautista's ship. With only a light breeze that night, both ships barely moved. But the *Pelican* didn't have the load Bautista's ship carried, so when Drake got within cannon range, he fired. The shot blasted the upper gunnels of the loaded ship, with chunks of wood and splinters flying everywhere, one of which hit Bautista. And before the Englishmen could reach the target ship, the wounded and stunned crew piled into their launch and rowed for shore. Drake pulled up to the abandoned ship, set his sailors on board, then both ships headed farther out to sea, away from the aroused Spanish port.

In Lima, Viceroy Luis de Toledo, who happened to be in the city, was notified at one o'clock in the morning that the English had just attacked the harbor. The Viceroy ordered the church bell rung, the alarm of the time, to assemble all the residents. After the assembly, 200 Spaniards with rifles boarded two ships and by ten o'clock the next morning they had started after the Englishmen. By that time, the *Pelican* and Bautista's ship had made their way about 15 miles out to sea, with the Englishmen pillaging through all of Bautista's merchandise.

Drake spotted the two ships coming, moving slowly because the wind was less than a breeze. He saw the Spanish ships riding high in the water, using only their lower sails—the Spaniards hadn't had time to load any ballast—and that made them hard to steer. But they were still closing the distance, so Drake ordered all the prisoners except for Nicolas Jorje put on Bautista's ship, and that included Juan the Greek, the pilot taken from the *Los Reyes*. Then he ordered his crew off the captured ship and the *Pelican* put full canvas to the breeze, setting a northwest course.

The two Spanish ships tried to follow the Englishman, but Drake slowly increased the distance from his pursuers. With the English ship on the horizon after only one day, the Spaniards turned their ships around and returned to Lima. The Viceroy was furious. His own son, Don Luis, and Pedro Sarmiento, second in command, explained that their ships didn't have ballast needed to use their topsails. Plus, many of the men were seasick and unable to fight. And also, they didn't have enough food to feed a crew of 200 men for a long chase. But they did save Bautista's ship and rescued the prisoners that Drake left onboard.

When pilot Juan the Greek reported to the Viceroy, he stated that the English sailed a solid ship with many cannons and carried a fighting force of about 80 men. So the Viceroy—after a temper tantrum—ordered that two ships be fully outfitted with 120 soldiers to hunt the Englishmen down. These two Spanish ships left Callao, Port of Lima, on February 27th; their chase will be picked up again later, before Drake exits the southern sea. In the meantime, the *Pelican* and the pinnace headed up the Peruvian coast on route toward Panama after Anton's ship loaded with silver.

3

The Silver Chase

Drake missed the silver shipments in Callao, Port of Lima, but he had another option. From information gained from Gasper Martin before the *Pelican* entered the major Spanish seaport, he knew Anton's loaded ship had left the port a day and a half before he arrived and that Anton planned to stop on route in the Port of Paita to take on flour. So the silver chase began, after the loaded Spanish galleon bound for Panama as the target.

Heading up the Peruvian coast, a trading vessel bound for Lima fell to the Englishmen, and after a quick search they found she carried nothing of value. The interrogation of the captain determined that he possessed no information about Anton's ship. So, the *Pelican* with full sail continued up the coast past Trujillo and arrived at the Port of Paita in late February. Once anchored in the harbor, Drake boarded a ship loaded with merchandise, from which he took 60 jars of wine and some wax. From this ship, Drake took a prisoner, Custodio Rodriguez. Rodriguez knew of Anton's ship and told Drake he had left Paita two days earlier. With this news, the *Pelican* and the pinnace caught the tide that night to make up time. On route, they intercepted the ship of Gonzalo Alvarez, from Panama bound for Peru. Nothing on board the ship interested Drake except a black Spanish slave, whom he freed and added to his crew.

Moving faster to make up two days, Drake passed into Ecuador. This country is known for old Inca stories of hidden gold and lost emerald mines. After the conquistadors defeated the Inca armies in 1563, Spain established an administrative district.

Off Los Quiximies between Cape de San Francisco and Cape Pasado, Drake stopped the ship of Benito Diaz Bravo. Bravo had just left Guayaquil bound for Panama. From his ship, Drake relieved Bravo of

40 bars of silver and some gold, one item being a gold crucifix. After a full search of the ship, Drake then threatened the passengers, who gave up hidden emeralds. Some of their emeralds were as long as a man's finger. Bravo's ship also carried rigging for an important fleet being assembled in Panama. This royal fleet would carry the new governor to Manila in the Philippines. Drake picked through all the rigging, took what he wanted, and dumped the rest overboard.

After that, the Englishmen took all of Bravo's food, a good amount of chickens and hams. Then they loaded the passengers along with Bravo's crew into the pinnace and ferried them to shore. Drake kept Bravo's black crew members, no number is given, just Negroes, possibly two or three. He also kept Bravo's clerk, Francisco Jacome, and sailed away. This left Bravo alone on his ship. But then something happened: After Drake sailed a short distance away, the *Pelican* turned around and headed back to the ship.

While on Bravo's ship the first time Drake questioned and played a few mind games with Bravo while his crew combed the ship from bow to stern without finding more treasure. But for some reason Drake thought Bravo had more hidden. Evidently, one of the black slaves freed from Bravo's ship told him that there was more gold and silver hidden away somewhere on the ship. Drake believed the maroon, because he had found other hidden booty on ships in Valparaiso and Arica. So Bravo must have a stash hidden somewhere, and Drake wanted it. And when he wanted something, he used extreme measures.

Once back on Bravo's ship, Drake threatened to hang him and his clerk if they didn't reveal where the rest of the treasure was hidden. When he didn't get the answer he wanted, he did just that. Bravo and Jacome were both strung up but were dumped into the sea before they passed out. Luckily for both, the crew in the pinnace fished them out and put them back on their ship. Then Drake ordered his crew to cut the sails down, which they tied to the anchor and let it drop. This left Bravo and his clerk adrift off the Ecuadorian coast as Drake sailed away with a small fortune in gold, silver, and emeralds, plus Bravo's black slaves. With full sail, the *Pelican* and the pinnace headed north after the slower moving ship of San Juan de Anton bound for Panama. This silver chase had started in Callao, Port of Lima, passed Trujillo, stopped at the Port of Paita, and traveled up the coast of Ecuador, having stopped four ships on course and covered over 500 miles.

The Treasure Harvest

On course for Panama to catch up with Anton's ship, Drake offered a gold chain as a reward for the first sailor to spot her. John Drake, the captain's young cousin, climbed high in the crow's nest and at about noon on March 1st, he spotted her moving slowly against the wind. Her location, about two days out of Panama.

The *Pelican* closed the distance fast, too fast, so Drake ordered wine pots dumped over the stern as a drag to slow the *Pelican* down. He didn't want to confront Anton in the daylight, so the *Pelican* hung back waiting for the sun to drop. The pinnace stayed astern of the *Pelican*, out of sight and loaded with a raiding party, until nine o'clock that night, when Drake cut the drag and pulled alongside Anton's ship.

Then the order was given for Anton to strike sail. He thought it was a joke and continued to forge ahead. He yelled back, "come and do it yourself, if you dare." So Drake gave the order to fire the culverin, a long-barreled cannon loaded with links of chain. The shot hit and wrapped around the third mast with such force that it took all the rigging over-board. At the same time, soldiers threw grappling hooks on deck, as a hail of arrows and harquebus shots struck the ship, one of which wounded Anton. Unknown to Anton, during the barrage the raiding party in the pinnace pulled around the side of his ship and used the sail lines to climb on board. The unarmed galleon fell fast, and with the ship secure, soldiers transferred Anton to the *Pelican*. Drake, clad in his thick leather suit, took off his helmet and greeted the stunned Spaniard, saying "have patience, for such is the manner of war." Then he ordered Anton locked up in the poop along with other Spaniards.

Author John Cummins, in *The Lives of a Hero*, speaks about the number of crew needed to operate Anton's ship. He submits that there were few Spaniards on board, indicating that "the ship's crew was composed largely of blacks or less likely of Indians." If Cummins is correct, then Anton's crew was mostly black. But there is nothing written that

Drake freed any of Anton's slaves and added them to his crew, as he did earlier and would do again later. So the total number of black slaves on Drake's voyage is questionable.

Anton's ship, a 120-ton galleon named the *Nuestra Senora de la Concepcion*, carried a heavy amount of treasure. But after her capture the darkness set in, too dark to see what she carried. Drake waited until the next morning to board her. He took inventory until about noon and then decided to take her farther out to sea, away from the coast. What worried him was the two Spanish ships from Callao that he thought could be following his route. He didn't know they had turned back to port to be outfitted with supplies and ballast needed for the chase. With the two ships lashed together and using the *Pelican's* sails, they moved slowly out to sea.

Once out of view of the coast, the crew started to unload Anton's ship, now nicknamed the *Cacafuego*. What this nickname meant before the capture was *spitfire*, but after the capture a young Spaniard on board changed the name to *Caca Plata*, meaning *Shitsilver*. Never had Drake seen such a prize; she was loaded with tons of silver, hundreds of pounds of gold, chests of coins, and countless jewels, all to support the whims of King Phillip of Spain.

No one knows how much treasure the *Cacafuego* carried, because part of the cargo had never been registered. What is known is that Anton's ship used silver bars as ballast, spread out along the bottom of the ship, plus what was loaded in her cargo holds. A 120-ton ship, to use full sails, needed at least 30 tons of ballast. In the cargo holds, with three different hatches, she could carry another 40 tons of goods. So Anton's ship could have carried as much as 70 tons of cargo.

The World Encompassed 1628 claims that Drake took 26 tons of silver from Anton's ship. Apparently, the 26 tons is wrong and the amount has been changed, as were other details about Drake's voyage. Elizabeth I kept the quantity of Drake's treasure a secret. The actual tonnage of silver Drake took will never be known, but it was a heck of a lot more than the reports claim.

According to H. R. Wagner, Drake's ship could carry 25 to 30 tons of dead weight in addition to the cannons, which weighed another 10 to 15 tons. Any more weight and the *Pelican* would have had trouble sailing.

And if bad weather happened, his ship could have serious problems.

Whoever figured the amount of silver that Drake stole used 35 to 40 pounds per bar, times 1300 bars, which comes out even and equals 26 tons. John Barrow, in *The Life, Voyages, and Exploits of Admiral Sir Francis Drake* (p. 47), claims that Anton's 120-ton *Cacafuego* could carry 26 tons of silver in ballast alone, not counting the cargo holds. The point here is that the amount of silver on Anton's ship far exceeded 26 tons, and Drake took it all.

Drake overloaded the *Pelican*. During the three or four days spent unloading Anton's ship, the crew of 80 or more men, plus Anton's slaves, dumped unwanted goods from the *Pelican* overboard to make room for the silver bars. Some items like pikes of tar, tackle, pickaxes, tools, and linen from belowdecks were left on Anton's ship. Prisoners who were locked up in the stern castle or poop observed through the vent holes the pinnace rowing back and forth from ship to ship, transporting silver. But there is no way the pinnace could have moved the full tonnage of silver in three or four days; that process would be too slow.

What the prisoners in the poop observed was partly correct. The *Pelican* had been grappled side by side to Anton's ship, with braided rope bumpers strung between the ships. The crew then set up a chain gang to pass silver bars from ship to ship and down into the cargo holds. What the prisoners observed when they saw the pinnace skirting the stern was the crew unloading a different area of the ship. Drake had enough crew, counting Anton's slaves, to unload the captured ship in more than one way, and everyone worked, even the gentlemen.

The *Pelican*'s crew in the same three or four days cleaned out all of Anton's food. On route to Panama, Anton had stopped over in the port of Paita to pick up flour. The amount is not given, but it had to be substantial, likely a few tons for the 120-ton galleon to have made the stop. Drake took all the flour and stored it in the hatch nearest the bow, next to the kitchen. So over the course of his travels, from every ship and port, besides a load of treasure Drake slowly added to the ship's food and wine supply, and he wasn't finished yet.

On March 6th, after dining with Anton and presenting gifts of gratitude to Anton's crew, Drake left behind two prisoners he had captured at the Port of Arica. They were Nicolas Jorje and a black slave who wanted to return to his master. Then he bid farewell to the *Cacafuego*. The crippled ship, about three days out of Panama, would have a slow journey to port and would be no threat of passing a message to authorities. The *Cacafuego* contained no ballast, riding high in the sea, had little or no food, and likely had only one or two usable sails. With the rear mast still hanging overboard, all the rigging would have had to be cut away before Anton could steer his ship or they would be sailing in circles with sail lines tangled in the rudder. Drake figured to be long gone by the time Anton made port.

With full sail, the overloaded *Pelican* and the pinnace headed north toward the Nicaraguan coast in search of fresh water. Evidently, Wagner was wrong when he stated that if the *Pelican* contained more than 30 tons of silver, she would have trouble sailing. It seems the *Pelican* had no problem sailing at all. Juan the Greek told the Viceroy in Lima that the English had a strong ship. What the Spanish didn't know is that the *Pelican* was a modified French galleon. As per a John Hawkins design, shipwrights had doubled her hulls sheathing and extended her keel, a forerunner for all English ships that would later fight in the 1588 war against Spain.

But along the course toward Nicaragua, the now slower moving *Pelican* started to leak. All wooden ships leak, but Drake knew he had a problem. With all the extra weight, the ship's lower seams started to expand, and more water than normal began to fill the bilge. He needed to quickly find a harbor where he could caulk the lower seams on his overloaded flagship.

R. J. Santschi, in, *Treasure Trails* (1937), wrote, "Drake, also called Red Beard and, by the Spaniards, El Draco, was a terror of the Spanish Main. Robbing Spanish ships along the coast of Peru, and sacking the towns, he accumulated so much plunder that his ships would not hold it all. To avoid danger of capsizing, he heaved overboard at what is now known as the 'Isle of Plate' bowls of silver money and tons of silver plate." Although his book is a good read, there are a few things wrong with the Santschi story. First, Drake only had one ship, not ships, at that point, and his ship would never capsize with that much silver ballast—it would go straight down. Second, nothing is written about any storms in the area at the time. All that extra weight had expanded the *Pelican's* lower seams, and "if" Drake dumped anything overboard, it sure wasn't his treasure. He had other heavy items that would go first, like part of his arsenal, heavy cannon balls or even a few cannons. And it should be said that modern-day treasure hunters are still searching for what Drake "may" have dumped overboard to lighten his flagship.

In a small bay on the Nicaraguan coast, opposite the island of Caño, Drake anchored the *Pelican*. Here he would stay, trying to figure out where to beach his ship to make the needed repairs. But with the load of silver on board, his ship drew too much water to get close enough to shore. What he needed was deep water next to the sandy beach, so he sent the pinnace skirting the shoreline taking depth readings. According to Wagner, the *Pelican* needed maintenance done anyway—the bottom cleaned—and that's why he entered the small bay. No, Drake was in a pickle; all the maintenance had been done earlier in Medio Cove within Salada Bay. At this point he was in trouble, and his voyage could have ended on the Nicaraguan coast.

Then Drake got lucky. He spotted a small ship, a bark sailing down the coast on route for Panama. He needed that ship to take weight off the *Pelican*. Immediately, a raiding party in the pinnace headed out after the unsuspecting ship. The bark belonged to Rodrigo Tello, who saw the pinnace coming but couldn't figure out who it could possibly be. Then orders came to strike sail, followed by a volley of rifle shots that sent the occupants heading for cover. The Englishmen climbed on board and once they secured the bark, sailed her back to the bay where the *Pelican* lay at anchor.

When the bark arrived, the first question Drake asked Tello and two pilots, Alonso Sanchez Colchero and Martin de Aguirre, is where he could find a harbor to work on his ship. When he didn't get a good answer, because no one seemed to know, Drake improvised. He decided to do the needed repairs in this small bay.

First, Drake ordered part of Tello's cargo, sarsaparilla, sent ashore. The bark also carried lard, honey, and maize that stayed on board. Then the cannons from the *Pelican* were off-loaded to the deck of the bark. English cannons were mounted on wheels, so they pushed them to where a block and tackle could swing them out and lower them onto the bark, about 10 to 15 tons in all according to Wagner. They handled heavy chests of Spanish gold and silver coins the same way. Then the silver bars were loaded in the pinnace and transferred to the beach. This lightened the *Pelican* enough that she could be brought closer to shore and tipped on her side to fill the failed seams. But the tides at the time did not ebb enough to expose the seams next to the keel. So the crew caulked and greased what they could above the waterline, one side of the flagship at a time, before they put her back in service. But the *Pelican* still leaked.

When Drake had sailed with the Hawkins fleet in the Caribbean and storm damage in the Gulf of Mexico had caused the *Jesus of Lübeck* to leak, Hawkins had sent carpenters down into the bilge to slow the leak down. So some repairs can be made inside the ship to control a bad leak, and Drake did the same with the *Pelican*, having his carpenters dam up what they could.

Two important prisoners had been taken from Tello's bark, the two pilots who were to take the new Governor, Gonzalo Ronquillo, to the Philippines. Earlier, before the capture of the *Cacafuego*, when Drake captured Bravo's ship, he had dumped most of the rigging for the new Governor's fleet overboard. Now he had the Governor's pilots, along with all their up-to-date navigation charts for the Pacific. To Drake, the charts were just as valuable as the treasure in the *Pelican*'s cargo holds. These charts gave him options for his escape from the southern ocean.

Contrary to what has been written about Drake loading all the stolen booty back on the *Pelican*, he did not. He didn't make the same mistake and overload his flagship again. That is what caused the crisis in the first place. He put as much weight on Tello's bark as she could carry, to take the strain off the *Pelican*'s hull, plus it made for faster sailing. Drake's prisoners had no idea what he loaded back onto the two ships, but they did see silver bars stacked all over the beach and noted that Drake used the silver bars as ballast. Otherwise, Drake locked them up while all activities were going on. Even in their later depositions to Spanish authorities, the prisoners could only account for their interactions with the Corsair and not what he loaded on each ship.

On March 26th, with excess weight on Tello's bark, the small fleet headed up the coast toward lower Mexico. On the 27th, the flotilla stopped. Drake put Tello and his crew in the pinnace along with a few supplies and set them adrift within view of the coast. But he kept

Alonso Sanchez Colchero, one of the captured pilots. Drake thought this pilot could direct him to the Port of Realejo. From information he gleaned, Drake knew that Spain had a ship under construction there for the Philippines trade. He claimed he wanted to enter the port and burn the ship.

Historians completely overlooked the real reason why Drake wanted to enter the port of Realejo. He had an alternative reason than to burn the ship—not that he wouldn't have carried that out too. Remember, when Drake wanted something, he used extreme measures to get it, and he wanted to enter the port in a bad way. Any facility capable of building a ship for the high seas would have a drydock or "ways" for repairing a ship. The *Pelican* still needed repair; she still had a bad leak or leaks in the lower seams. Drake planned to take over the port, set up artillery to protect the area, and then repair his flagship. With that type of ship-building facility, he wouldn't even need to unload his ship to make the repairs. But Colchero wouldn't cooperate. He said he didn't know how to enter the port. So Drake strung him up, trying to force the information, but that didn't work, and while Colchero struggled and twisted on the rope, they dropped him on deck. So the plan to enter the port failed and the repairs on the *Pelican* would have to wait.

Moving farther up the coast of New Spain, the crew spotted a small ship off the starboard, and before daybreak the next morning the distance between the ships began to close fast. Not knowing what was about to happen, the pilot of the small ship yelled out an order for the *Pelican* to "get out of the way," but the answer came in a volley of rifle (harquebus) shots, along with the order to strike sail.

Once on board, the raiding party took over the ship and continued to sail her up the coast. One of the passengers turned out to be a VIP, Don Francisco de Zárate, a cousin to the Duke of Medina, a rich feudal landowner in Spain. Drake had a long conversation with him about who he knew and whether anyone on board was related to the Viceroy. With little information acquired, Drake searched his new prize. He found expensive merchandise from China—silk, linen, and porcelain. He pillaged what he fancied, and from Zárate he took a unique item, a falcon of gold with an emerald mounted in the breast. Then, after a three-day ordeal, Drake replaced the pilot Colchero with a Portuguese sailor named Juan Pascual, who he thought could find him fresh water. And after he thanked Zárate and presented small gifts to Zárate's crew, Drake took Zárate's personal Negress and sailed away, leaving the ship without any provisions or water casks.

According to Wagner, Drake intended to head for Acapulco to burn any ships that could cut off his escape route. Maybe, or again did Drake have other intentions, like fixing his leaking flagship? But from his conversation with Zárate, he found out that Acapulco was well armed and he would have to fight to take that port. Drake wasn't about to take any chances in a port where he would have to fight when his flagship and the bark were loaded with Spanish booty. So on April 13th, he made his last port stop, the harbor of Guatulco in lower Mexico. The first observation of the port showed only one ship at anchor, so the *Pelican* and the bark entered the harbor around noon with a raiding party ready to head ashore.

Guatulco only had a few houses and a church. The commerce of the small town exported native products, mostly clothing from the surrounding area. The townsmen were preparing for holiday festivities when the *Pelican* entered the harbor. So a few curious residents went down to the beach to welcome what they thought were the vessels transporting the new Governor, Gonzalo Ronquillo, to the Philippines. But as the launch loaded with soldiers came within view, one of the sailors on the beach recognized the landing party as Englishmen. By the time they could sound the warning and retrieve any weapons, smoke rose from the *Pelican*'s deck and cannon balls started whistling into the village. The explosions scattered everyone in the town, with most running for the woods, as the raiding party landed.

Soldiers armed with swords and shields headed into the town. Once there, they ransacked everything and took anything of value. Like in Valparaiso, they even packed away the church bell cast in silver and destroyed all religious artifacts. Four Spaniards who failed to escape were rounded up and transported back to the *Pelican*. One prisoner was the local pastor, along with his two relatives; the fourth, Gomez Rengifo, Drake needed to lead him to the watering spot. Drake also used Rengifo as an intermediary between the captain of the Spanish ship anchored in the harbor and his sailors onshore who had fled into the woods. Drake needed firewood, so he threatened to burn their ship unless they brought him the wood.

In a house by the harbor, the raiding party found 25 water kegs and some earthen jars. Including the water kegs already on the *Pelican*, Drake now had enough water to last 50 days, and longer if they collected rainwater. To make room for the extra water and native goods found on the Spanish ship, the crew threw unwanted or old food into the harbor. They also restocked the ship with a new supply of festive food collected from the town.

Before leaving Guatulco, Drake released all prisoners, including Nuño da Silva, the Portuguese navigator and ship owner captured off the Cape Verde Islands. He also added to his crew one black slave freed from the town. Then on the evening of the Holy Thursday, April 16th, the leaking *Pelican* and the bark, both loaded with riches of New Spain and South America, left the harbor of Guatulco, bound for the high seas.

4

The Mystery Begins

After leaving the harbor of Guatulco, Drake disappeared into the South Pacific. Most recorded accounts say he sailed directly into the sea for 500 leagues, others claim 600. Directly into the sea means he sailed west, the fastest way with the wind out of New Spain. The coastline of lower Mexico runs to the west, so after heading to deep water he kept the land in view. But there is something missing in this part of Drake's voyage, and most writers leave this part out. No one has figured out how the stolen bark and his leaking *Pelican*, both loaded with treasure, could possibly sail at the same speed to cover 100 miles a day. The two ships could not. The bark was a coastal trading vessel not set up for the high seas. The small ship only had two masts and traveled slowly.

What is missing in this story is that Drake had no need for the small bark once he had sailed safely out to sea. Drake had a secret, a deception that only his crew knew about. Spain would not obtain this information until 1587. That is why Drake had overloaded the *Pelican* after he captured the treasure-laden *Cacafuego*: He thought his ship could carry the extra weight for a short distance. But he proved himself wrong when the strain on the *Pelican*'s hull started popping the lower seams. That forced him to seek out the bay near the Island of Caño to make repairs. That is why Drake needed Rodrigo Tello's bark, for a pack boat, just for a short time, because he had another ship awaiting his arrival out at sea. Yes, he had another, larger ship waiting.

Drake's Deception

Drake learned from experience in the Caribbean that the fastest and most undetectable way to maneuver along the coast required only one ship and a pinnace. The main reason for his tactic is that a fleet drew attention, but one ship on the horizon or entering a harbor appeared commonplace. And he didn't want to draw attention; surprise for him worked the best. So, after he missed the 500 silver bars at Chule, Port of Arequipa, he knew he had to change his mode of action to stay ahead of the Spanish warning system. Drake needed to change to his Caribbean strategy the rest of the way up the South and Middle American coasts. To that point, Drake had the charts from three ships commandeered from Valparaiso to Chule, and he knew the layout of all the ports at least from Valparaiso to Acapulco. Therefore, off the coast of Chule, Port of Arequipa, he had turned three captured ships loose with full sails, with Spanish prisoners out on deck as witness. Drake purposely wanted the prisoners to see the event; otherwise, they were kept locked up in the poop. The ships released were the small ship taken from Chule, the small ship taken from Arica, and the large ship taken from Valparaiso. Drake's deception was that he had left a skeleton crew belowdecks on the *Los Reyes* or the *Grand Capitana*, taken from Valparaiso.

Once the *Pelican* and the pinnace sailed away toward Callao, Port of Lima, the hidden crew on the *Los Reyes* had orders to lag behind, stay out of view of the coast, and meet the *Pelican* at a predetermined location. The meeting spot was off the lower Mexican coast. The sails on the *Los Reyes* were already deployed, so all the skeleton crew needed to do was navigate to their destination and then tack around and wait for the *Pelican*.

As stated earlier, Spanish ships sailed more slowly than English ships. They had poor steering and the superstructure stood higher than on English ships. They were built bulky. For this reason, Drake sent the *Los Reyes* out to sea as his backup ship while he and his fast-moving landing craft went in search of Spanish treasure.

The Spanish spotted the *Los Reyes* heading up the coast one week behind Drake. Pedro Sarmiento received this information after he left Callao, Port of Lima, on the second chase to hunt down the Englishmen.

On the first chase, the two Spanish ships were forced to turn back to Callao because they had no ballast to use their topsails. Nor did they have supplies to feed 200 men. Plus many of their crew were seasick and unable to fight if they did confront the Corsair.

On the second Spanish chase in search of Drake, Sarmiento states,

> … when we arrived at Santa, we found that the Corsair had passed by fourteen days before, and that off the port of Truijillo he had captured a vessel belonging to one Cataro and had taken from it what he wished, so that we left at once for the port of Truijillo, as we had news that six days before, there was a large ship there with a sprint-sail, which was believed to be the pirate. (Wagner, *Sir Francis Drake's Voyage*)

A sprint-sail flows out off the ship's bow, with a hole sown in it to let the water spray out as it dives through the waves. Only large ships, like the *Pelican* and the *Los Reyes*, had a sprint-sail. Again Sarmiento, searching the shipping lanes, states, "It so happened at this same place we saw a sail [not a sprint-sail] and with the news which we had, we went up to her to look her over, but it turned out to be a merchant ship."

From Sarmiento's account, Drake had passed by two weeks before, then another large ship with a sprint-sail was spotted a week later. The second large ship, a week later, was the *Los Reyes*, lagging behind and heading for lower Mexico to meet up with the *Pelican*. The sail Sarmiento spotted was not a sprint-sail. He states that it was just "a sail," and likely one of many smaller merchant ships in the shipping lanes out of Panama bound for southern ports.

Sarmiento, who later became a writer, had no idea at the time or even later that Drake had kept the *Los Reyes*. He would have recognized the ship if he had seen it, because he was second in command of her on an earlier voyage to the Solomon Islands. Juan the Greek, the pilot of the *Los Reyes*, reported that Drake had turned his ship loose with full sail and no one on board. No Spaniard would know about Drake's deception until the capture of his young cousin John and his second interrogation in Lima, Peru, later in 1587. Not only did Spain discover that Drake kept this noted ship. They also found out, from John Drake, the degrees for Drake's North American landing site. Later, in the 1600's,

Spain would use the name of this stolen ship in their fabricated voyage of Admiral de Fonté.

Evidence to support that Drake kept the *Los Reyes* comes from Spanish prisoners who took a count of Drake's crew. No one knows for sure the number of crew members aboard the *Pelican*. Different prisoners had different counts. One prisoner claimed 86, but another, named Nicolas Jor Je, a Fleming native of Ansuyque, claimed 71 or 72 men.

Nicolas Jor Je witnessed the release of the *Los Reyes* and two other smaller ships off the coast of Chule, Port of Arequipa. Drake wanted him to see the three ships set adrift with no one on them, but Jor Je saw more than that. His low crew count of 71 or 72 men confirms missing crew members. The missing crew was hidden on the *Los Reyes*, along with any black slaves freed to that point. Plus, Jor Je saw what Drake's crew took off the ships before their release, and if one follows the wine—a very important commodity to Drake and his crew—something is telling about why Drake kept the *Los Reyes*. He needed the storage. The Fleming Jor Je, speaking about the *Los Reyes*, stated that "Drake took out wine and other things, but left much of the wine and much of the lumber." Jor Je's statement supports the fact that Drake kept the *Los Reyes*, because most of the countless jars of wine, over 1500, were stored on the ship, along with the lumber for firewood. And Drake would never dispose of those two needed commodities.

Another important piece of evidence from Drake's voyage to support that he kept the *Los Reyes* comes from when the pinnace captured the bark of Rodrigo Tello and took her to the cove near the Island of Caño. At that time, Drake had a conversation with his new prisoners about his voyage and his ships. Mrs. Nuttall, in *New Light on Drake* (p. 113), states that Drake claimed to have another ship larger than his own sailing alone out at sea with more artillery. He also claimed to have two smaller ships sailing up the coast. The larger ship sailing alone out at sea was the *Los Reyes*, heading to meet the *Pelican* off the lower Mexican coast. The two smaller ships were the *Elizabeth* and the *Marigold* that disappeared in the storm when they entered the southern Pacific. Drake did not lie; he presumed his other two lost ships were coming up the coast. But more important, from Drake's own statement, he had a larger ship than his own sailing alone out at sea. This confirms he kept the *Los Reyes*.

On the same page of *New Light on Drake*, Spanish prisoners are said to have claimed that Drake's flagship had a rating of 200 tons. Of course their estimate was wrong. The English used small ships and the *Pelican* was only 100 tons. H. R. Wagner claims the *Pelican* was a 120-ton ship. So who is right? Spanish prisoners exaggerated the details when questioned, but what is important here is that the Spaniards also claimed the *Los Reyes* was a 200-ton ship, like the *Pelican*. There is no way to know from any records where the Spanish built the *Los Reyes*, or her real size. What happened is, the Spaniards exaggerated the size of both ships. What is known is that the *Los Reyes* was a larger ship than the *Pelican,* but not twice the size. So a reasonable deduction is that the *Los Reyes* was 120 tons and the *Pelican* was 100 tons.

Drake needed the *Los Reyes* but didn't want the Spanish to know he had kept her. He employed a deception off the coast of Chule, Port of Arequipa, when he left a skeleton crew belowdecks when orders were given to let her go with the wind. And he gave the hidden crew orders to meet the *Pelican* off the coast of lower Mexico. Drake kept this celebrated Spanish ship, and she is the second ship, disclosed later by young John Drake, taken on the northern voyage to the new country Drake named Nova Albion.

The Voyage North

From Guatulco in lower Mexico, the leaking *Pelican* and the stolen bark of Rodrigo Tello sailed directly into the sea, to the west. Along this route, about a week's sail out of Guatulco, Drake met up with the stolen *Los Reyes.* At their predetermined location, all the treasure and native goods from Tello's bark were off-loaded to the *Los Reyes* and the bark set adrift. Drake then lightened the *Pelican*'s load to take excess stress off the hull, taking into consideration that both ships needed to sail at the same speed, more or less, 100 miles a day.

With the up-to-date charts for the Pacific taken from Alonso Sanchez Colchero and Martin de Aguirre, who were assigned to take the new Governor Gonzalo Ronquillo to the Philippines, Drake kept on course to the west. From the captured charts, he knew the return route of Spanish ships along the California coast. The Spanish ships returning from the Philippines only sailed within view of Cape Mendocino before turning south to New Spain. Along the coast they used the California current, a strong current that in some stretches runs eight miles an hour. Drake needed to sail west through and beyond this cold southerly current before he could make any course change.

No California Landing

Most historians believe that Drake landed in northern California, above San Francisco, at Point Reyes. All the literature claims he sailed north to 48°, around Washington State, then turned back south to 38° 30 min, where he spent five weeks working on his two ships. His California landing never happened; someone in the English government, like Sir Francis Walsingham, spymaster for Elizabeth I, changed his landing degrees by ten to keep Spain from knowing where he really sailed. And his orders to change the degrees came directly from the Queen. Elizabeth I held personal reasons for this deception that will be covered later.

Drake knew the direction of the trade winds from having sailed to the Caribbean. He sailed south to Africa to catch the westerly winds and then north up the Florida coast to catch the easterly winds. From this knowledge and the stolen Spanish charts that showed the Lower California coast trending out to the northwest, he stayed on course to the west for 600 leagues (1800 miles). Then he had a choice to make. First, to continue on across the Pacific to the Spice Islands, or second, to go in search of the narrow passageway of Anian, a northern route back to England, as shown on the Ortelius Map. He chose the latter.

After sailing 600 leagues to the west, Drake turned magnetic north and didn't changed course for another 1000 leagues (3000 miles). When he passed California, his ships were over 250 miles off the coast and heading straight for the Gulf of Alaska, 1600 leagues in all. His journey followed a wide "V" shape, not the dotted lines on later maps that show him heading up the North American coastline. The coastal route for his ships would have been impossible because the California current flows south along that course. Plus, his supposed route north to 48° and then back south to northern California doesn't match the documented 1400 leagues in all, that also had been altered by 200 leagues from 1600 leagues or 600 miles. Furthermore, there is no bay in California at 38° 30 min where he could have landed, but there is a hidden bay at N 48° 30 min where he did land. Drake didn't land in California; his route took him straight into the Gulf of Alaska.

Voyage to Alaska

From *The World Encompassed 1628,* "we were neerer on it then wee were aware." Heading magnetic north, Drake's ships headed straight for the Alaskan coastline and right into a terrific storm. "The ship's lines iced up, the crew was freezing and the wind was howling. When the wind died down the fog set in, then the wind would start again blowing the fog away." With freezing air temperatures and moisture in the air, ice will form on anything exposed to the weather, and that is what happened to Drake's ships. All the sails and rigging iced up. This icing-up problem still happens to ships today. Crab fishermen heading to the Bearing Sea with pots stacked high on deck have iced up, making them top-heavy and causing the ship to flip over, with all hands lost.

The current in the Gulf of Alaska runs in a counterclockwise circle between the warm Japanese current that streams toward the Bering sea and the cold California current that flows back south toward the tropics. Drake encountered contrary winds and a howling storm from the west. The Alaska current, also wind driven, pulled his ships to the northeast. He ran for the shore and found a bay, where he found no protection:

> In this place was no abiding for vs; and to go further North, the extremity of the cold (which had now vtterly discouraged our men) would not permit vs: and the winds directly bent against vs, hauing once gotten vs vnder sayle againe, commanded vs to the Southward whether we would or no. (*The World Encompassed 1628*)

From where his ships were in the Gulf of Alaska, they could observe land running farther out to the west, as if to meet Asia: "The land in that part of America, bearing farther out into the West" (*The World Encompassed 1628*). There is only one place on the Alaskan coastline where the land runs to the west, and that is the area east of Prince William Sound; beyond that, around Cook Inlet, the coastline starts to dip to the southwest.

One noted English gentleman, Thomas Blunderville, who published his work in 1592, claimed (because he had heard) that from a bay at 46°, Drake sailed much farther north to look for a strait, the narrow passageway of Anian (Wagner, *Sir Francis Drake's Voyage*). These rumors heard by Blunderville were half right. Drake never entered a bay at 46°, but he did sail farther north in search of the Strait of Anian.

The two ships fought a raging storm in the Gulf of Alaska on June 5th, 1579, around N 58°. At that time Drake could not take a correct latitude reading, so he may have even been farther north. While in the gulf, they observed the mountain range to the west that was 3000 to 5000 feet high and inland from the coastline. Mount Saint Elias looms in the area to the west and towers over a mile high. The mountains along the Alaskan coast are what Drake's crew observed when they saw land trending out to the west.

The *Pelican* had been leaking before they reached Guatulco in lower Mexico, forcing a repair on a sandy beach near the Island of Cano. But the tides were not low enough to get at the bottom seams. After the long journey of about 4800 miles into the north Pacific, with the unsuitable weather and heavy load of treasure, the *Pelican* developed a big problem. With all the diving and twisting through the icy cold Pacific in the Alaskan storm, the unfixed lower seams opened even wider. With 45-degree water leaking into the bilge and his crew hardly able to move, they still had to man the pumps. Facing another dilemma, Drake had no choice but to turn his ships back south.

Voyage Back South

Desperate to find a place to work on the *Pelican*, his ships turned south and followed the shoreline looking for any suitable harbor, but the land along this stretch of coastline is all rock. Even if they had spotted a favorable bay, the tides in Alaska in the month of June run like rivers. Alaska even has bore tides, some of the largest in the world. On an incoming tide a wave or wall of water six to ten feet high rushes into the empty bays at 10 to 15 miles an hour. Working on the *Pelican* in the Alaskan bays, because of 20-foot tides and extreme weather, was out of the question.

As his ships proceeded down this windswept rocky coastline of Alaska, the crew observed a bird nesting. The bird had to be big enough to see from the ship, so it was either an eagle or a blue heron. These weather-hardy birds build a large sticky nest atop any barren half-dead tree. Because eagles fiercely protect a large nesting area, the heron nests near the eagle for protection. Along the journey they observed trees with no leaves. The trees were the giant conifers, Douglas fir, western red or yellow cedar, and hemlock; they have needles, not leaves, and are green year around. The only conifers found in the British Isles are in the Highlands of Scotland, the Scottish pine. It is apparent that none of the English seamen knew what to call these strange trees, so they stated they had no leaves.

Drake had a fast ride south with the wind off the stern and the tides running like a river. He skirted the islands of Southeastern Alaska looking for any bay to make needed repairs. After they passed the Alaskan panhandle, his ships turned east into Dixon Entrance, a wide east-west passage on the northern end of the Queen Charlotte Islands. These islands today are known as Haida Gwaii. Drake then sailed east into the Hecate Strait toward the high rugged Canadian coastline, where he turned south into Queen Charlotte Sound. Still heading south along the western Canadian coastline, his ships entered Queen Charlotte Strait at the southern end of Queen Charlotte Sound.

Whether Drake intended to enter Queen Charlotte Strait or the strong tides pulled his ships south will never be known. But one thing is certain, by following this course so close to the coastline, he was desperate to find a harbor to work on his leaking flagship. However it happened,

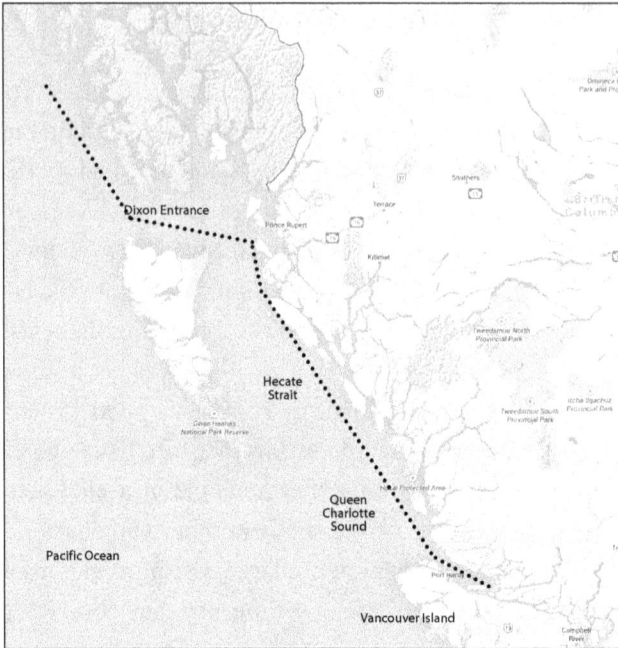

Drake route (dotted line) overlaid on background of base map.

Map data ©2014 Google.

his loaded ships ended up in the Johnstone Strait, between Vancouver Island and the mainland of British Columbia.

Captain George Vancouver in 1792 charted this inside waterway. The wide channel flows between high snow-capped mountains on both sides of the strait. The main channel flows along the east side of Vancouver Island, with islands and side channels toward the mainland. Vancouver's ships, the HMS *Discovery* of 337 tons, along with the *Chatham* of 131 tons, using launches, worked their way up every side channel, taking reading of depths, latitude, and longitude. As stated in his journal, Captain Vancouver found the Johnstone Strait and Discovery Passage, at the southern end of the strait, to be very passable but with one tricky section. The ebb tides south moved fast, about seven to eight miles an hour. The flood tides north flowed more slowly, about four to five miles an hour. At times, they experienced gale-force winds and downpours of rain. When he finished the survey up these two passageways for roughly

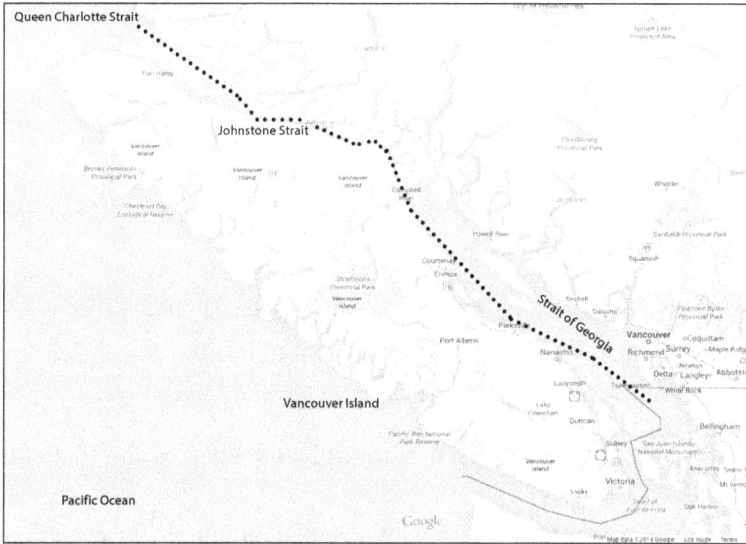

Drake route (dotted line) overlaid on background of base map.
Map data ©2014 Google.

85 miles into Queen Charlotte Strait, Captain Vancouver's comments were as follows:

> Little remains further to add respecting the station we had just quitted, but to state the general satisfaction that prevailed leaving a region so truly desolate and inhospitable (Meany, *Vancouver's Discovery of Puget Sound*).

Drake followed the Johnstone Strait south along the eastern side of Vancouver Island, which points to the southeast. The Johnstone Strait ranges in width from about one and a half to three miles. At the southern end of the strait, Drake entered Discovery Passage, a dangerous stretch of water 16 miles long and about a mile wide. In the lower half of the passage, the waterway is less than a mile wide at Seymour Narrows. When Drake passed through this deadly section of the passage he somehow missed Ripple Rock in the narrows. This submerged twin-peak mountaintop lay nine feet below the surface at low tide and today is the graveyard for 120 ships. In 1958, miners burrowed under the rapids and filled the peaks with explosives. Then Ripple Rock disappeared in the largest nonnuclear blast in North America.

At the southern end of Discovery Passage, Drake entered the Gulf of Georgia, also called the Georgia Strait and lately renamed the Salish Sea. Here, Drake entered the North Puget Sound, named by Captain George Vancouver in 1792. Once below the 49th parallel, he entered today's American waters:

> From the height of 48. deg. in which now we were, to 38. we found the land by coasting alongst it to bee but low and reasonable plaine. (*The World Encompassed 1628*)

Clearly, this passage has been changed by ten degrees and should be N 58° to N 48°.

Drake's ships left the high snow-capped mountains surrounding the Johnstone Strait and passed through Discovery Passage into the Gulf of Georgia. At that point he entered a channel 10 to 30 miles wide and observed a low plain of land. In Canada, this area is called the Lower Mainland, and in the United States, it is named the Georgia Basin or the Puget Lowlands.

Drake followed the Georgia Strait southeast, the natural flow of the channel, toward the mainland. He sailed into a vast inland sea with the mainland off his bow and lush green islands in every other direction. On this route southeast he left the largest island he had followed south, Vancouver Island. But the high mountains of this large island still loomed off his stern to the west. As he sailed southeast in the Georgia Strait for 138 miles, he drew close to the mainland. About 15 miles away his ships spotted a high landmark off the port side, Point Roberts, with steep white cliffs. Off his bow, to the east they observed two other landmarks with steep white cliffs, Birch Point on the north and Point Whitehorn on the south, of which the latter connects to high steep banks that run south as far as the eye can see. Between the two landmarks off his bow, Drake caught sight of a bay with a gray sandy bottom:

> In 38 deg. 30. min. we fell with a conuenient and fit harborough, and Iune 17. came to anchor therein. (*The World Encompassed 1628*)

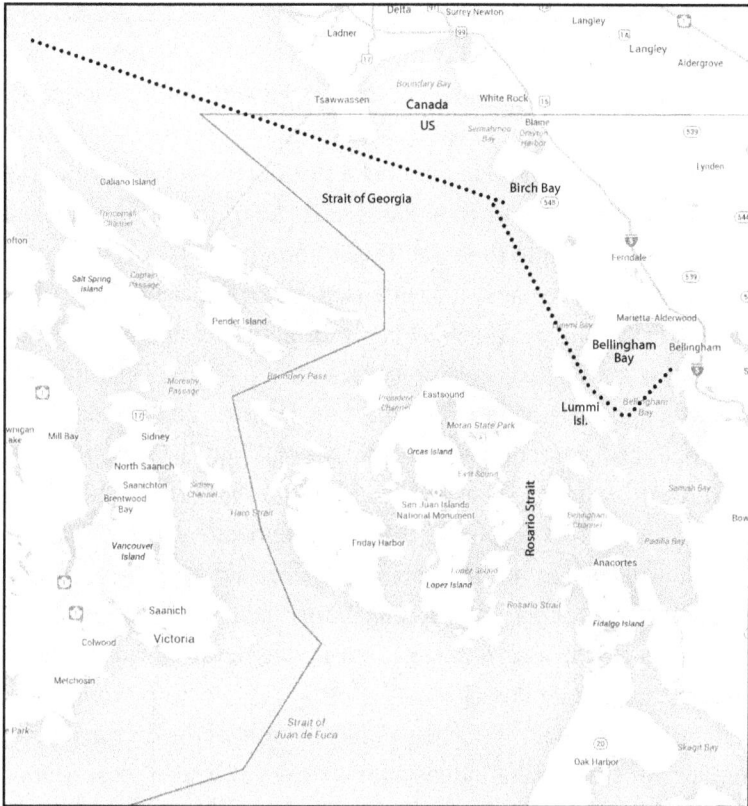

Drake route (dotted line) overlaid on background of base map.

Map data ©2014 Google.

Drake Lands Within N 48°

With a good southerly wind to enter the bay, Drake's two ships dropped anchor in today's Birch Bay, just below the 49th parallel in the North Puget Sound. But Birch Bay is not Drake's Bay that historians have searched for, as drawn on the Portus Map.

Birch Bay is Drake's "conuenient and fit harborough," as written in *The World Encompassed 1628*, or "a fair and good bay," as written in *The Famous Voyage,* but the degrees, after being corrected by ten, are not N 48° 30 min. These degrees are wrong because Drake landed in three different bays, and the 48° 30 min refers to the third bay he landed in, not Birch Bay.

The traveling time south took 10 to 12 days; Drake left Alaska on June 5th, then landed in Birch Bay on June 17th, 1579. The notes of Francis Fletcher, the ship's pastor and naturalist, claimed a 14-day journey. For Drake to have sailed this inside route speaks a lot to his skill as a navigator. He definitely gambled in uncharted waters sailing south through the lower section of the Inside Passage, as he followed the eastern side of Vancouver Island to the inner Puget Sound.

Navigators, historians, and authors claim Drake could not have sailed this far north. Climatologists using information from the study of tree rings claim a mini ice age and icebergs filled Queen Charlotte Sound 430 years ago. It is true that in the 16th century glaciers did advance in Europe, and winters were extremely cold, but that didn't happen in North America until 1711 to 1724 and 1824 to 1835 (Lamb, 1977, p. 435). During these two events in the Western Hemisphere, the ice only grew at high altitudes and in the Arctic Ocean but did not affect the Gulf of Alaska or Queen Charlotte Sound. Ships have struck icebergs in the channels of Southeastern Alaska, but Drake never sailed through that section of the Inside Passage.

Even 20,000 years ago when glaciers a mile high advanced in North America, the Queen Charlotte Islands were not affected. These islands are known as the Canadian Galapagos. Scientists worldwide still study the different species of plants and animals in Haida Gwaii. So the claims that it was impossible for Drake to have sailed this far north are unfounded.

So far, from Drake's last port stop in Guatulco, Mexico, loaded with Spanish treasure and a stolen Spanish ship, the *Los Reyes*, he set his coarse in a wide "V" shape. He first sailed west through the California current for 1800 miles (600 leagues) to clear the North American coastline. Then he crossed over to the easterly wind flow, heading magnetic north straight into the Gulf of Alaska. After a terrific storm in the gulf and contrary winds, he abandoned his effort to find the fable Strait of Anian. And from a latitude of N 58° he then turned south, followed the coastline of Alaska to Dixon Entrance, entered the lower Inside Passage, and passed the 49th parallel into American waters. The first of three different bays where he landed is today's Birch Bay on the mainland. His journey from lower Mexico to the new country he named Nova Albion had covered roughly 5400 miles in about 56 days.

5

Nova Albion

The sea on most days is calm, nothing like the swells of the open ocean, but alive with the tide ebbing and flowing. Blue herons dot the shoreline looking for a meal while the call of seagulls and seabirds squall in the distance. A cool breeze flows onshore over a large gray tide flat, with a hint of rotting sea grass in the air. Inland around the bay grew giant fir and cedar trees 20 feet around that towered 300 feet in the sky. This forest blocked any view of the interior landscape with massive green foliage unlike any forest the Englishmen had seen before.

Drake anchored in his "conuenient and fit harborough," on the mainland in today's Birch Bay at 48° 55 min, a lush green country with hundreds of small and large islands within view. To the south were the San Juan Islands, to the west the Gulf Islands of British Columbia, and also to the west in the background looming high on the skyline 30 miles away, Vancouver Island, the large island they had followed southeast along the Johnstone Strait.

From this harbor three landmarks clearly stood out: Point Roberts, to the northwest about ten miles away, with high white cliffs that taper down into Boundary Bay along the 49th parallel; to the north Birch Point, with steep white cliffs that make up the northern side of Birch Bay; and on the south side of Birch Bay, Point Whitehorn, with steep white cliffs that can be seen from 20 miles away on a clear day. Attached to Point Whitehorn are high vertical banks that, from Drake's vantage point in Birch Bay, appeared to run to the southern skyline:

> This country our generall named Albion, and that for two
> causes; the one in respect of the white banks and cliffes, which
> lie toward the sea: the other, that it might have some affinity,

euen in name also, with our owne country, which was some
time so called. (*The World Encompassed 1628*)

In this description of Drake's new country, the writer or narrator made
a small mistake and transposed the description of the terrain: "the white
banks and cliffes" should be "the white cliffes and banks." The cliffs are
white when seen from a distance; the vertical banks range in height from
about 300 feet around Point Whitehorn to half that height farther south
and are a dull gray with large white boulders scattered along the beach.

Once both ships anchored in Birch Bay, the *Pelican* needed imme-
diate attention, and either they had no time to take a reading of latitude
for Birch Bay or the overcast weather normal for this country covered
the sun. One important point here is that Drake had taken the Inside
Passage south searching for a bay where he could work on his leaking
flagship, and he figured the work could be done in Birch Bay, his "conuenient and fit harborough."

On the third day Drake brought the leaking *Pelican* closer to shore
to unload goods. But first, something happened on the second day. The
natives of the country showed themselves. They sent out a brave in a
canoe chanting and waving feathers, which will be covered later. The
native presence did make a difference to the Englishmen, because they
had no idea at the time whether the natives were friend or foe. From their
experience with natives in South America, they weren't about to take
any chances. And the native presence made a difference in Drake's plan
to unload goods on shore.

Following the order of events stated in *The World Encompassed 1628*,
they built a fort and set up tents. None of these activities happened in
Birch Bay. But they will happen in another bay, a second landing site
about a week later.

The month of June not only has the longest days of the year, it also
has the lowest daylight tides of the year. Drake's crew spent the first and
second day unloading cannons and goods onto his second ship, the *Los
Reyes*, until she was full, as he had done with the stolen bark near the
Island of Caño. At the same time, Drake took note of the low tides in
Birch Bay and sent the launch to check the deep channel that runs north-
south in the bay. This channel is a long way out from the beach. On the

low June tides, the ebb drops about half the total distance of the bay, with a massive tide flat exposed. When the two ships had entered Birch Bay, they anchored in the outer reaches of the bay, on a line between Birch Point and Point Whitehorn, in about seven fathoms (or 42 feet) of water. Drake planned to use the north-south channel in Birch Bay to repair his leaking *Pelican*. So after his crew unloaded everything possible onto the stolen *Los Reyes*, they still had more goods to offload on shore. On the third day the *Pelican* headed closer to the beach. But what direction did he take and what part of the beach did he plan to land on? Because of the native presence on shore, Drake took the *Pelican* out of Birch Bay and left the *Los Reyes* behind.

At this point, the narrative of *The World Encompassed 1628* about Drake's flagship ends and it goes into first European contact with Native Americans. Something happened. The story has a big hole in it, as do all other accounts of his Nova Albion landing. What happened in the "conuenient and fit harborough"? Here, one has to fill in the blanks of what happened to Drake's *Pelican* when it left Birch Bay. The following three points come from my many years of commercial fishing in these waters. First, Birch Bay is not Drake's Bay, as shown on the Portus Map. Second, because Drake landed in three different bays, he had not found the other two bays yet; they are miles away, and he had no idea of their location. Both of the other bays, farther south, are hidden. The third point is, Drake would never have sailed his ships south to where the other bays are located without exploring the way first; the tides at the time were too fast and the narrow channels of the San Juan Islands lie in that direction. And Drake would never have sailed into what looked like a dead end, and that is what a southerly route from Birch Bay appeared to be from his vantage point.

The following is what happened in Birch Bay, left out of *The World Encompassed 1628*. Early in the morning just before daybreak on the third day, Drake used the ebb tide that drops southwest towards Point Whitehorn. If he had gone out into the Georgia Strait too far, the ebb tide would have taken him to the west toward Vancouver Island, so he kept the *Pelican* just off the southern rocky point. His plan was to anchor his ship on the south side of Point Whitehorn, away from any possible native attack. He would anchor in deep water and unload his cargo onto a sloping beach with a few boulders lying around, just below the high white cliffs. Then he could use the flood tide back into Birch Bay where he planned to work on his ship. Then once the *Pelican* had been repaired, he could use the same ebb tide to pick up his goods again. But disaster happened and his flagship started taking on more water than the pumps could handle. Drake's flagship started to sink on the south side of Point Whitehorn, in the Georgia Strait.

With the power of the incoming tide, which runs like a river on the lowest tides of the year, the anchor would never hold a ship filling with water. The anchor would even help suck a filling hull farther down as the tide drug the sinking ship right back into Birch Bay. How fast the *Pelican* went down or what the crew salvaged will never be known, because the English narrative left out all accounts of what happened in this first bay where Drake landed in Nova Albion.

With the overloaded *Los Reyes* still anchored in Birch Bay, Drake had important decisions to make. First, what route to take to get through the southern islands? He dared not sail the *Los Reyes* any farther south from Birch Bay without exploring the narrow passageways between the San Juan Islands first. So he left the Spanish ship behind and with a crew set out in a launch to explore a deep-water route through the southern maze of islands, roughly eight miles away.

The native Semiahmoo lived in Birch Bay and had showed themselves. They had sent out a canoe, at high tide, with one of their braves chanting and waving feathers. Because of their experience with the natives in South America, the crew readied their weapons. But these natives seemed peaceful and showed no threat, so some of Drake's crew took a trip ashore to fill their depleted water barrels. This contact with the Semiahmoo happened while the launch headed south to explore a route through the San Juan Islands.

This first landing after two months at sea occurred along Terrell Creek, a freshwater source about 15 to 20 feet wide and running parallel to the beach for about a mile before entering Birch Bay. While there, the crew checked out the native campsite, hidden behind the giant fir trees, and observed that "their houses were built round with cliffs of wood close to the earth and very warm" (*The World Encompassed 1628*), a trademark of the Coast Salish. Thus, the first European contact with Native

Americans, a tribe known as the Semiahmoo, happened in Birch Bay. There is no account of Drake being at this first contact with the native Semiahmoo in the "conuenient and fit harborough." He had left in a launch to explore a way through the southern islands.

About five days passed and the launch returned to Birch Bay. On their exploration they had followed the high banks south of Point Whitehorn and discovered hidden behind the cliffs, about eight miles south and not within view of Birch Bay, a long sand spit whose beach dropped into deep water. This long sandy beach, named Sandy Point, is the northern peninsula of today's Lummi Bay. At that time a major river, the Nooksack, entered Lummi Bay from the east and spilled out into the lower Gulf of Georgia. The timeline for the launch being gone comes from the notes of Pastor Francis Fletcher. He claimed that on the eighth day goods were brought to shore. Fletcher's account, like other reports, left out the sinking of Drake's flagship. But his account of the eighth day landing is correct, as is the account of the *Pelican* being brought closer to shore on the third day to unload goods. These two events happened in different bays, about a week apart.

As the explorers in the launch returned to Birch Bay, their venture found deep water all along their southerly route. Drake then left his "conuenient and fit harborough" and used the ebb tide that runs south close to shore. He let the overloaded *Los Reyes* drift along the high banks that *face the sea*, past Cherry Point, past an inlet known as the Gulf, to what today is called Sandy Point, named from the charts of the Wilkes Expedition of 1841. Without knowing, the Englishmen left the territory of the Semiahmoo people in Birch Bay and entered the land of the Lummi tribe.

At Sandy Point, on high tide late in the afternoon on the eighth day, Drake's crew pulled the *Los Reyes* close to shore and tied her off to *trim the ship,* meaning clean the bottom. On shore, the crew packed one of their small cannons up the beach and built a fort or a gun turret, to protect the ship while it was hopelessly laid up on the beach. This action supports the fact that Drake only had one ship at Sandy Point. If he had had a second ship, he would have stationed it in the lower Gulf of Georgia for protection and wouldn't have needed a fort.

He had a similar plan while in Birch Bay, to use his second ship for protection, but disaster happened and he lost his flagship.

From Drake's fort his men could hear natives coming down a trail, but the natives could not see the fort. Drake's soldiers built their fort on the north end of Sandy Point, where the high banks and the giant tree line stopped and the sand spit begins. Today that trail where the natives were heard is a steep gravel road that drops down to Sandy Point less than 100 feet east of the beach.

Lummi Bay at 48° 46 min is Drake's second landing site in Nova Albion. Here he tipped the *Los Reyes* on her side to clean the bottom for faster sailing. Ships that sail in the southern oceans need the bottom cleaned twice a year, whereas in the colder northern waters cleaning is needed only once a year. The bottom of the *Los Reyes* had not been cleaned since before her capture in Valparaiso, Port of Santiago, and must have been dragging a lot of grass, barnacles, and slime. Due to the sandy beach dropping into deep water, the crew didn't have to tip the ship at a sharp angle, only enough to expose the keel. They cleaned one-half of the ship's bottom at a time, turning the ship around at high tide to repeat the process.

At Sandy Point, the Lummi chief came to visit. The Englishmen called him *Hioh*, but what the Englishmen had heard was a native ceremony and not the name of the chief. They heard the "hi, hi, hi, oh, oh, oh" performed with drums beating before the chief arrived. These natives had a ceremony for all important events, and the Englishmen claimed they carried on for half an hour.

In the meeting the Lummi crowned Drake as a great chief and Drake, in turn, performed a Protestant service. The Englishmen observed that the native chief wore a fine deerskin, setting him apart from the others. The chief really wore a sea otter skin, not a deerskin. Coast Salish held sea otters in such high regard that only top officials of the tribe could wear them. The native women, not knowing what to expect of these visitors from the sea, clawed at their faces until they drew blood. They wore only a deerskin around their waist, so Drake gave them garments pilfered from the ship in Guatulco to cover their bosoms.

On the beach where the crew was working on the *Los Reyes*, they observed natives never failing to take a fish. One can only imagine the millions of salmon milling around in the lower Gulf of Georgia, going through a change to fresh water before darting up the river. The Lummi are clever fishermen and today still fish the Nooksack River. But in those early years the Lummi used fish traps. They strung lead lines out from the beach and anchored them in the river. The lines would then collect sea grass, which would create a wall and direct the salmon into a cage where they could be scooped up. That is why Drake's crew observed the Lummi never failing to take a fish.

While waiting for the tides to change, Drake's men hiked inland to check out the country. They followed a trail along the south side of the Nooksack River, or "Drake's Estro" (estuary), into the Ferndale Valley. A few miles up the river was the territory of the Nooksack tribe, who lived and fished along the river. In the estuary, full of small islands and backwaters, where the river meandered and the water backed up at high tide, they saw all the needs of man. They spotted birds, deer, elk, and a strange kind of "conie" (a muskrat).

Today the Nooksack River no longer flows into Lummi Bay where it emptied into the lower Gulf of Georgia. Around 1888, when loggers dropped the giant old-growth trees into the river, a massive log jam collected that changed the river's course and the fishery of the Lummi tribe. Also, where the Nooksack River once meandered throughout the Ferndale Valley, the area has been claimed for farmland and dikes hold the river in check as it flows into another bay, Bellingham Bay. In the late 1800's "Drake's Estro" disappeared.

While at Lummi Bay, Drake had a treasure to protect, and the lower Gulf of Georgia is a wide-open location, not Drake's cup of tea. He needed a hiding place. At this point he spent another week at Sandy Point trimming the *Los Reyes*, making it two weeks total in Nova Albion. But he didn't just sail away from Sandy Point to a third bay. The sand spit is protected from the wind. Lummi Island, shown on the Portus Map and the most easterly of the San Juan group, blocks the wind in the summer. Looking out from the beach where the work on the ship took place, toward the north end of Lummi Island, the water is flat and shiny. So Drake needed to wait for the ebb tide and use the outflow of the Nooksack River to leave his second port stop in Nova Albion.

Drake's Bay

After the *Pelican* sank in Birch Bay, Drake scouted the area south and found a deep channel through the San Juan Islands that led to a hidden bay. From Sandy Point, Drake's *Estro*, once the ship had been trimmed, Drake used the ebb tide and the outflow of the Nooksack River for his next destination. The *Los Reyes* drifted south past Gooseberry Point, into a long north-south channel named Hale Passage. The ebb tide moves fast through this glacier-carved fjord, and Drake steered his ship to deep water on the western side of the channel. He drifted with the ebb tide the full length of Lummi Island.

On the east side of the channel, about halfway through Hale Passage, the *Los Reyes* passed a long peninsula. At this location the land to his left is flat and at water level. At high tide the land is underwater, which makes the southern section an island, called Portage Island, but on the ebb tide it shows an uninterrupted peninsula. As Drake drifted past this low section, he could look east into the northern end of the hidden bay. The loaded ship stayed in deep water and drifted the full length of Hale Passage. At the southern end of the passage is where the wind returned, and Drake turned the stolen Spanish ship east into today's Bellingham Bay, named by Captain George Vancouver in 1792.

Bellingham Bay is "Drake's Bay" as shown on the Portus Map. Officially named the *Portus Nove Albionis*, this old map is the only piece of documentation of Drake's North American landing that is known to exist. (See page vii.) Even with the Portus Map, historians have been unable to locate Drake's Bay, because the map has little detail nor a regard for size. That is because the Portus Map is a second-hand source.

Judocus Hondius, a Dutch engraver, spent time in England and sketched Drake's Bay from a drawing hanging in the government buildings at Whitehall, in London. He then added his sketch, as an inset, to a larger map called the Hondius Broadside. The Hondius map depicted the voyage of Francis Drake and Thomas Cavendish. Another writer of the time, Samuel Purchas, also saw the picture of Drake's Bay in the Whitehall Gallery and said the drawing, made by Drake's young cousin John, looked distorted. Still, Judocus Hondius saved a part of history that could have been lost forever, because later, the Whitehall Gallery burned to the ground.

What Hondius failed to capture on his Portus sketch is that the island—Lummi Island—next to the peninsula has a high rounded mountain on the south end that tapers down to high banks on the north end. The lowest land on Lummi Island is on the west side, on the northern half of the island. Hondius did get the shape of both ends of Lummi Island correct, although the island is actually longer and thinner, but it was still recognizable as a whole to a commercial fisherman. However, it was the flat spot on the east side of the Portus Map, the site of old Fort Bellingham, that drew my attention. Then, the rest of the map followed suit. The distance between Lummi Island and the mainland, in Hale Passage, is 0.8 of a mile, where today the Washington State Ferry uses the protected waterway from Gooseberry Point to the island shown on the Portus Map.

Once the *Los Reyes* caught the wind at the southern end of Lummi Island, the most easterly of the San Juan group, Drake sailed her east into Bellingham Bay and anchored in a small bay within Bellingham Bay, named Harris Bay. While in Harris Bay the overcast weather cleared and he took a reading of latitude of 48° 30 min. Captain George Vancouver in 1792 named and charted Bellingham Bay at 48° 36 min. Here Drake would stay for three weeks making plans and collecting provisions for his long journey back to England.

Harris Bay, on the south side of Bellingham Bay, is not shown on the Portus Map. This small bay where Drake anchored is protected from the predominant winds and sits behind a landmark called Post Point. While at anchor, the *Los Reyes* was hidden from any possible Spanish ships sailing into the main entrance of the bay, from the southwest. Well hidden, Drake didn't worry about any Spanish ships retracing his route from the north through Hale Passage, because there was no wind for a ship to use. Plus the channel appeared too narrow for any enemy ship to consider.

In Harris Bay Drake remained in Lummi territory. The tribe had no permanent settlements on the bay itself, although on the Portus Map, huts appear on the northern skyline. The native Nooksack tribe, who lived inland along the Nooksack River, used Bellingham Bay to collect shellfish, and the Samish tribe, who lived on the islands to the south-west, would paddle by on their way to other destinations. The native tribes of the area called Harris Bay *Seeseetichenl* or *Seeseelichl,* which interpreter Hilaire Crockett translated as "quiet place where something good is always found or floats in." What the natives referred to is an eddy that forms in Harris Bay, created by Post Point as the tide flows into Bellingham Bay. Good or bad, the eddy also collected Francis Drake, where he found a great hiding place.

So far in Nova Albion, Drake had encountered four different peaceful native tribes while moving south from Birch Bay to Bellingham Bay. *The World Encompassed 1628* has these tribes all lumped together as one, but they had different names and protected territories.

Harris Bay is where Drake's dreams of grandeur kicked in. With the *Los Reyes* ready for sea, he renamed the stolen Spanish ship as the *Golden Hind.* On Post Point, where he had stationed a lookout for Spanish ships, they spotted an outcrop of rock that would be a great place to construct a monument to claim this new country for England.

Post Point has a great view of the main entrance to the bay and the San Juan Islands to the southwest. "The Islands were within view" (*The World Encompassed 1628*). The point itself is a sandstone formation, a part of the Chuckanut formation that develops into high steep cliffs far-ther south. This location, about a quarter of a mile from the anchored *Golden Hind,* clearly stood out. At the time, the sandstone outcrop dropped down from a high bank, where it tapered to sea level and jetted out into the bay. The location, although different now, at that time had a small bay on each side of the point, with the surrounding land covered in giant old-growth fir trees 300 feet tall. So Drake constructed his monu-ment with a backdrop of green on an outcrop of stone that overlooked inner Bellingham Bay.

Today the point is not as impressive as it was when Drake viewed it. The railroad has cut through the sandstone cliffs and filled their roadbed with large cinder blocks, boulders, and gravel. But using one's imagina-tion to reconstruct the area, it is possible to see why Drake picked Post Point to construct his monument. In 1579, the point stood alone, clear of giant fir trees and visible to anyone who sailed into the bay.

Drake's Monument

> Before we went for thence, our generall caused to be set vp,
> a monument of our being there; as also of her maiesties, and
> successors right and title to that kindome, namely, a plate
> of brasse, fast nailed to a great and firme post; wheron is
> engrauen her graces name, and the day and yeare of our arri-
> uall there and of the free giuing vp, of the prouince and king-
> dome, both by the king and people, into her maiesties hands:
> together with her highnesse picture, and armes in a piece of
> sixpence currant English monie, shewing it selfe by a hole
> made of purpose through the plate: Vnderneath was likewise
> engrauen the name of our generall & c [crew].

Most historians, after reading this passage from *The World Encompassed 1628*, presumed that Drake's "great and firm post" left in Nova Albion was his monument, and that the post must be wood, with a brass plate nailed to it. They also presumed that after four centuries of weathering, any trace of Drake's monument would be gone. Wrong.

Drake carved his monument in stone. On the east side of Post Point on a high outcrop of Chuckanut sandstone are vertical cliffs that rise about 15 feet above the gravel beach. On the vertical cliffs, Drake's crew built scaffolding around a pointed section of the cliff face. One of the scaffolding holes on the east side is still visible today. Then, with a drawing made by young John Drake, the crew chiseled out a Renaissance carving, not of the Queen as stated above, but of King Henry VIII and his sixth wife, Katherine Parr, with "armes in a piece of sixpence" (arm in arm). Drake's carving depicts a wedding ceremony, with the six-pence representing good luck. The old English saying about the four "somethings" a bride should carry actually ends with a fifth item—"a sixpence in her shoe."

In the carving, King Henry has his thumb in his right breast pocket and is wearing his wide-brimmed hat, as in some of the portraits of him (viewable at luminarium.org). Today, he is missing his head, found about 40 feet away all rounded from rolling around in the waves on stormy days.

The carving of Katherine Parr has long flowing hair that runs horizontally, with her most notable trait, big breasts, as in her portrait in the Weidenfeld and Nicolson collection. Katherine Parr is the only one of King Henry's six wives who displayed these two noticeable characteristics.

The vertical cliffs with Drake's glorious creation wasn't visible to the southwest entrance of the bay, only to the inner bay. So his crew chiseled out a "great and firm post" about 10 to 12 feet long from a wave-cut section of sandstone in a crevasse by the water's edge. A long section of cut sandstone still sits in the crevasse today. After the mason cut and trimmed the long post, the men drug it up the slippery embankment and mounted it high above the carving. Drake's "great and firm post" cut from Chuckanut sandstone stood high above Post Point, visible to anyone

sailing into the entrance of the bay. And below the post sat Drake's monument carved in stone to claim his new country for England.

When the stonemason who carved Drake's monument finished his work of art, he chiseled his initials high on the rock face. His initials are "RI" with a "C" halfway above the other letters, then a "W." His name is Richard Cadwell, found on an old English document in the book by Mrs. Zelia Nuttall, *New Light on Drake*. All the other names of Drake and his crew, according to *The World Encompassed 1628*, were carved under the monument. But the carving is no longer attached to the high cliff face; it now lies on the beach. And it didn't just fall down, someone blew it off the cliff face, and that started the search for "who did it" that will be covered later.

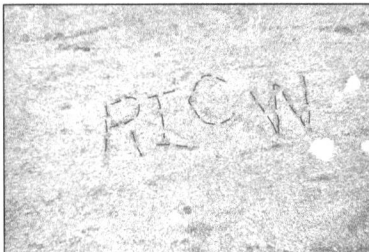

Photos taken by the author in 2000.

Photos taken by the author in 2000.

The chisels for such a large project need to be sharpened, and on a sandstone knob about 30 feet away are numerous X-shaped marks. These crisscross indentations were once deep, but the knob is exposed to the direct weather, which has worn down the surface to where the marks are hard to recognize.

Photos on these next pages were taken by the author in August 2014.

Damage and weathering have taken their toll. The post is no longer there.

Brass Plate

Once Richard Cadwell finished the stone carving, he gave it a thick coat of paint that Drake's crew called, "a plate of brasse." This paint, or "brasse," was a product used by the Spanish for bottom paint on the *Los Reyes* to keep woodworms from burring into the hull. The paint originated in the mountain mining districts of South America, where the Spaniards rendered down toxic mine waste that contained copper, lead, and zinc. On Drake's double-sheathed *Pelican*, grease was used on the hull. Nuño da Silva, the Portuguese pilot, claimed Drake's ship did not have a copper bottom, nor did she use ballast. Any copper products in England needed to be imported and were very expensive. But in the gold mining districts of South America, copper leaches and other minerals ran freely in mine water. This copper paint is dark red and came from the stolen *Los Reyes*.

In the statement from *The World Encompassed 1628*, "shewing it selfe by a hole made of purpose through the plate," the word "hole" is spelled wrong; it should be whole—the whole carving was showing itself through the "brasse." Drake's brass plate preserved much of his monument from erosion that normally would have erased many of the clues after 430 years.

Why did Drake choose King Henry VIII and his sixth wife Katherine Parr for his monument? That is a good question. Possibly because King Henry had broken with Roman Catholic influence in England, but during his reign he never accepted the Protestant religion either, so what the heck was Drake thinking?

When Queen Elizabeth I discovered what Drake's monument represented, because she confiscated all of his logs that contained the drawings, she was likely displeased, because this was her realm, not her father's. What she thought of King Henry, no one knows. She likely blamed him for the death of her mother, Ann Boleyn, executed on trumped-up charges. Elizabeth's favorite saying was, "see and keep silent," and she did. King Henry had banished both of his daughters, Mary and Elizabeth, from the monarchy; he wanted a son, which he got, Edward VI. Katherine Parr, Henry's sixth wife, was the only real mother Elizabeth had known.

It was Katherine Parr who had reintroduced both daughters to their father and helped to put them back into the line of succession, but after Edward. To King Henry, their reinstatement meant nothing, because his son would become king. So Elizabeth I hid or destroyed all the information about Drake's famous voyage and Nova Albion; she didn't want Drake's monument to be known to anyone. Plus all the crew were sworn to secrecy under penalty of death. Elizabeth I, during her lifetime, until 1603, never allowed any publications of Drake's voyage. And the Queen's wishes to hide Drake's new country carried over even after her death.

Whoever wrote the passages in *The World Encompassed 1628* and *The Famous Voyage* either knew of the Queen's displeasure about Drake's monument or were directed to change the wording to honor the Queen and not King Henry. The statement reads, "both by the king and people, into her [should be *"his,"* meaning King Henry's] maiesties hands: together with her highnesse picture [meaning Katherine Parr's], and armes in a piece of sixpence [arm in arm, representing a wedding ceremony, with the sixpence for good luck] currant English monie." Drake's dreams of grandeur about his new country—and his dedication—fell to pieces when his Queen disapproved of his monument.

Furthermore, another reason why Drake may have dedicated his new country to King Henry is that he didn't know whether his Queen still lived. His voyage lasted three years, and the first thing he wanted to know upon his return to England was, how goes the Queen—he wanted to know if the Queen still ruled. Looking back to before Drake started his famous voyage, Pope Pius V had proclaimed the Queen a heretic and ordered an assassination or a change of government. The monarchy of England was under attack, but survived, and Drake's dedication of Nova Albion to King Henry VIII means he really screwed up. And thus began the cover-up ordered by Elizabeth I.

Drake's monument no longer sits in its splendor on the rock face at Post Point. In 1790, a Peruvian in the Spanish Navy blew it off the cliff face and destroyed the "great and firm post" visible from the southwest entrance of the bay. Where the Peruvian placed the powder under the monument and lit the fuse is the same place where Drake and his crew had signed their names. When the blast went off—heard for miles if it was enough to break solid rock—a large piece from underneath broke and flew out, landing about ten feet away.

As luck would have it, on that piece of rock is Drake's sign of authority, a hand with a pointing index finger. Today that section of rock is underwater at high tide. In the fall, as the sun travels south, sea grass grows on the displaced chunk. Then in the spring, as the sun returns and the tides start to drop in the daylight hours, the heat cooks the grass and the incoming tide washes the grass away. During that small window in the spring, on a sunny day, the camera captured what the naked eye cannot see, the "plate of brass" that once covered Drake's whole monument. Later, when the heat of summer arrives, the copper and other mineral colors fade to white, and all the beach rocks blend together.

With the picture enlarged, next to Drake's hand is the date 1579, along with a circle that shows crisscrossed lines within, as seen on a Spanish or English coin. Then, well worn but still visible are two swing lines that match the way Drake signed his name.

On the back side of the three-ton carving of King Henry VIII and Katherine Parr, wedged between the wall rock and the

Top two photos taken by author in 2000, bottom photo taken in 2014.

carving is a four-foot section of his "great and firm post." This piece of post is bleached white from standing high in the sun for over 200 years and does not match the dark gray wall rock where it sits today. The four-foot piece of post appears to be the top of the once 10- to 12-foot-tall landmark. Other small broken pieces about a foot long are also in the area around the carving, but nothing that looks like the base. The lower section of the post is where a plate, "fast nailed to the post," would be found. A Peruvian in 1790 busted off that section of post as proof and reward that he had discovered the lost harbor of Francis Drake.

Exit From Nova Albion

As Drake's stay in his new country ended, five weeks total, he made important decisions about the long journey home. Because his flagship the *Pelican* had sunk and with the now *Golden Hind* overloaded, he left crew behind with a promise that he would return in one year.

The campsite where part of Drake's crew, along with an uncertain number of blacks, waited was next to a small creek named Padden Creek. The area is along the waterfront, down the hill from today's historic town of Old Fairhaven, a southern suburb of the present-day City of Bellingham.

Mrs. Nuttall, in her book *New Light on Drake*, toiled through old English records and claimed that Drake had returned home with only 50 men. She determined that he had left 21 men and 1 woman behind in Nova Albion. We do know the woman was black, but how many other blacks he left is unanswered. Following Drake's raid up the South American coast, he had freed black Spanish slaves from ports and from captured ships. Out of all the black men, only one asked to be returned to his owner. Furthermore, there is no account of Drake freeing any black slaves from the ship that should have had the most, the Spanish treasure galleon *Cacafuego*. So the total number of men left in Nova Albion could have been much higher than in Mrs. Nuttall's account.

There is only one reason why Drake left crew behind in this new country. His flagship, the *Pelican*, had sunk, and the *Los Reyes*, renamed *the Golden Hind*, didn't have room with all the treasure that Drake had amassed.

While anchored in Harris Bay and with the activities going on at Post Point, Drake sent a launch to explore a route to the open Pacific. For seamen able to read the tides, Bellingham Bay, or Drake's Bay, is easy to interpret. On the flood tide there are tide streaks, small rip tides, all in a line one after the other, as the ocean pushes in. The route the crew explored using the ebb tide pointed southwest toward today's Bellingham channel that connects to the southern end of the Rosario Strait. From the Rosario Strait the ebb tide pulled them out into the eastern end of the Strait of Juan de Fuca, about ten miles wide, which connects to the open Pacific 90 miles away.

The day before leaving, Drake took the *Golden Hind* out of Harris Bay on the flood tide and anchored her out in the center of the bay to wait for the ebb tide the next morning. Because the tide starts to drop before daybreak, he needed a reference point to keep the ship in the channel. On the Portus Map of Drake's Bay, a person is seen on the peninsula with a fire to guide the departing ship. Drifting with the ebb tide before daybreak, the *Golden Hind* cleared Point Carter and Eliza Island on the south end of Lummi Island, all shown, except for Eliza Island, on the Portus Map. At daybreak, with the tide moving fast, the *Golden Hind* passed between Cypress and Guemes Islands, in today's Bellingham channel. By then, Drake had plenty of light to steer his ship into the southern end of the Rosario Strait. At the end of the tide, about six hours after his departure, on the 24th of July, the *Golden Hind* anchored again:

> Not farre without the habrough did lye certaine Ilands, we called them the Ilands of Saint James, hauing on them plentifull and great store of seales and birds, with one of which wee fell July 24, whereon we found such prouision as might competently serue our turne for a while. (*The World Encompassed 1628*)

The certain islands where the *Golden Hind* anchored to hunt seals and birds are a maze of islands called the San Juans, all 170 of them. Drake laid over off Lopez Island at the eastern end of the Strait of Juan de Fuca on his two-day journey to the open Pacific.

The Puget Sound has over 300 species of birds and a lot of fish-eating seals. Where Drake anchored is on the flyway of birds heading to Dungeness Spit on the south side of the Strait of Juan de Fuca, now a bird sanctuary. As for seals, any commercial salmon fisherman will tell you that seals love gill nets and will clean out a net fast, leaving only a few heads behind. Today seals are protected from fishermen, and their population has grown.

In the summer, with clear weather in the North Puget Sound—haying season—warm dry winds from the northeast blow through the Frazer Canyon in Canada and out across the Strait of Juan de Fuca. Drake used this wind, a tail wind, to sail to the open Pacific. If a weather front had been moving onto the coast, he would never have made the 100-mile trip in two days, because the *Golden Hind* would have needed to tack all the way. So the *Golden Hind* sailed from Drake's Bay, between two islands, into the Rosario Strait. Drake then sailed south, skirting the southeastern San Juan Islands, into the Strait of Juan de Fuca and out to the open Pacific in two days. Thus, "the islands were within view, but a two day sail."

Now with a slower moving ship, the *Golden Hind*, he could only cover around 50 miles a day because of the load of treasure. At the mouth of the Strait of Juan de Fuca, Drake set his course SSW toward the Spice Islands. The SSW course comes from the *Anonymous Narrative*, a manuscript in the British Museum dictated by some of Drake's crew who had been sworn to secrecy. Who better to know the course than the seamen on the *Golden Hind*. If this course had been followed from his supposed California landing, Drake would never have found Indonesia or the Spice Islands—he would have ended up somewhere south of Australia.

One important account of Drake's voyage comes from a distinguished English naval officer who knew Drake, Sir William Monson. He collected Navy documents and published his work. H. R. Wagner claims that what Monson published was full of mistakes, the result of careless reading of Monson's manuscript when the book was printed, because of where he said Drake sailed:

> In the course of this he says, but lastly, and Principally, that after so many Miseeries and Extremities he endur'd, and almost two Years spent in unpractis's Seas, when reason would have bid him sought home for his Rest, he left his known Course, and ventur'd upon an unknown Sea in 48 Degrees,

which Sea or Passage we know had been often attempted by our Seas, but never discover'd (Wagner, *Sir Francis Drake's Voyage*).

Sir William Monson had tried his hand as a privateer, but had no luck. He knew Drake, and after the famous voyage, they teamed up to search for Spanish ships that had sacked the Port of Penzance. So his account of Drake sailing in a sea at 48° is correct, and the information Monson gleaned came from Drake himself.

Drake would have a long, slow journey home, halfway around the world, but not without incident. Other historians have covered this portion of his voyage, trying to figure out why his ship, an English ship with cannons, wasn't spotted on route. Their question cannot be answered, because Drake sailed a Spanish ship home.

The rest of Drake's story will be covered as it fits into later battles and voyages—mainly the names that were assigned to his new country, and why they are wrong.

The new country Drake discovered in 1579, within N 48°, held all the needs of man. Peaceful natives crowned him as a great chief and shared their hospitality. But who were these natives, and why don't they recall the visitors they once welcomed?

6

Natives of Nova Albion

The waterways were their highways, hunting and fishing their subsistence. Dugout war canoes would chase northern invaders from local waters. Upon entering their territory, visitors would back up canoes and wait for permission to come ashore. When they saw Drake's giant sailing craft for the first time, it sent panic through their world, so they hid. On the second day they showed themselves and sent out a canoe to investigate.

English seamen made first European contact with Native Americans in Birch Bay, in the Northern Puget Sound. These native peoples, the Semiahmoo, lived in Birch Bay and are classified as Coast Salish, with a sub-classification of Straits Salish, because of a dialect difference.

The Semiahmoo had a large territory, from Birch Bay north, all the way around today's Boundary Bay, ending at Point Roberts. Much of their domain ran above the 49th parallel, on the Canadian side of the border.

In 1792, when Captain George Vancouver charted Semiahmoo territory, his surveyors observed giant beams over 14 feet in the air, the full length of the beach at Cannery Point, on Point Roberts. The beams were all that remained of a large encampment estimated to house over 1000 natives. The observation left the surveyors wondering how they ever lifted the beams so high.

Cannery Point has a shallow reef that salmon need to cross when coming out of Boundary Bay heading for the Frazer River, in Canada. The summer fishery supplied the Semiahmoo with a good portion of their winter provisions. So before Europeans arrived, millions of wild salmon supported the Semiahmoo, as the fish passed over the shallow reef on Point Roberts.

In later years, early American companies operated two fish canneries on Point Roberts, a Pacific Alaska Fishery on the east side, where the Semiahmoo fished, and another on the west side, but residents I spoke to could not remember the company name. An old-timer who grew up on the point recalled a concrete slab and old stories that the cannery used Chinese labor.

The Semiahmoo did not fare well with the influx of Europeans. First, the smallpox epidemic spread by early Spanish exploration lowered the populations of all tribes. Then after Captain Cook's 1778 voyage to the Pacific Northwest, fur traders began to arrive on northern Vancouver Island. They traded guns for furs to the northern tribes, who in turn raided south into Semiahmoo territory.

By the time American settlers began to arrive in the 1850's, the Semiahmoo numbered only about 300, with their population continuing to dwindle. At last count, the Semiahmoo numbered only 24 members in four families living in Canada. But when Drake landed in Birch Bay, the Semiahmoo greeted the first Europeans.

As Drake moved the stolen *Los Reyes* from Birch Bay to the sand spit at Lummi Bay, he entered the land of the Lummi tribe without knowing it. The name Lummi comes from the word *nuglimmi*, meaning "people." The Lummi also had a large territory, running from south of Birch Bay to Bellingham Bay (Drake's Bay) and then west to San Juan Island, the most westerly of the San Juan Group. On San Juan Island, overlooking the Strait of Juan de Fuca, they were known as the Songish/Lummi.

The Lummi have lived in the North Puget Sound for thousands of years. Their estimated population when Drake arrived was no more than 3000. They also have the classification of Coast Salish, with a sub-classification of Straits Salish. The Lummi language is the same as that spoken, with dialectic variation, by the Samish and Klalam to the south, the Semiamu to the north, in British Columbia, and the Songish, Sanetch, and Sooke on Vancouver Island, also in British Columbia. Their neighboring tribes were the Semiahmoo, from Birch Bay north, and the Nooksack, inland along the Nooksack River.

Materials from the giant old-growth forest and sea fulfilled the Lummi's basic needs. They were boatbuilders, tied fishing nets, and constructed houses of permanent wooden frames, covered with hand-split cedar planks. In their long houses they only burned alder so as not to cause sparks that could burn them down. In the rafters where the smoke rolled through, before escaping out a hole in the roof, they hung items to be preserved, like meat, oysters, and salmon. In the old-growth forest a fungus once grew that the natives used as we use a potato. When loggers devoured the giant old-growth trees, an important supplement of the natives' diet disappeared.

The Lummi did have local enemies, but the greatest threat to all the southern natives came from the north. One northern tribe who terrorized the south practiced cannibalism. The head-hunting Yukylta, of the Kwakiutl group, from northern Vancouver Island, received firearms first and changed the balance of power in Nova Albion. When they raided south with newly acquired weapons, the Semiahmoo built forts near the present-day city of Blaine for protection. But once the Hudson Bay Company moved into British Columbia, a transformation occurred and the Yukylta claimed they lost their spiritual power.

Other invaders who lived even farther north were the Haida from the Queen Charlotte Islands or Haida Gwaii. The Haida continued to raid south even as settlers began to arrive in the late 1800's. This prompted the British to send a warship north to stop the raids. After cannon volleys bombarded the villages of Haida Gwaii, turning night into day, the raids south stopped.

From stories told, the Lummi/Songish on San Juan Island, before Europeans arrived, crossed the Haro Strait on raids up the Sannish Peninsula, a part of southeastern Vancouver Island. But the Lummi also had trade routes, one of which ran to the eastern end of the Frazer Valley, in Canada, home of the Sto:lo people. The Sto:lo traded with tribes on both sides of the Cascade Mountains. On these trips, the Lummi bartered tightly woven hats, baskets, and delicacies like smoked oysters. In return, they received chert for arrowheads and sacred ochre, yellow to orange in color, which they used for paint.

Every year the Lummi have a get-together called the Stommish. Natives come from all areas of the Puget Sound to celebrate and trade wares. One exciting event of the Stommish is the war canoe races. Each of these long, sleek canoes is chiseled out of one old-growth cedar log and can carry a dozen warriors. In the early years the Lummi used war canoes to catch up with northern invaders who raided their territory.

In a conversation with a stocky, well-spoken Lummi named George, a linguist preserving his native language, I asked the following questions:

How did you get the name George?

> George: The Lummi signed the Point Elliot treaty in 1855, which assigned tribal reservations, and then all school-age children were taken away to boarding school. There, all the children were lined up along the building and given a name. That's how I got the name George.

With all the different tribes in the Puget Sound speaking a different dialect, how did natives communicate?

> George: We could always understand neighbors next to us and they could always understand neighbors next to them, so when something went around, it spread in a chain reaction.

Why did the Haida come this far south on raiding parties?

> George: They were just like the Vikings, they came to pillage and plunder. Go look at where they live (Queen Charlotte Islands); it's nothing but a big rock.

The Semiahmoo lived next to the Lummi; how did they get along?

> George: Other tribes that lived next to the Lummi were just suburbs, just like city's today have suburbs.

When I asked George questions about who the natives referred to as the "Old Salish" might be, he had no answers. Why don't these local natives remember such an extraordinary event as Drake's arrival in their territory in 1579? George did refer me to the Pacific Northwest Studies, but that too only went back to the late 1700's. What happened?

American settlers and the smallpox epidemic wiped their history slate clean. Natives of the Pacific Northwest in the area of Drake's landing used oral history, passed down from generation to generation. When the smallpox hit, out of the thousands who had once lived around Drake's landing, only a small number survived. In the late 1800's, a count of natives on the Lummi Reservation revealed only 900 souls.

The smallpox epidemic also hit the northern tribes hard. The Haida on the Queen Charlotte Islands, or Haida Gwaii, also lost thousands of population. A count there after the epidemic also determined about 900 souls. And along with the epidemic went much of their culture and their history.

American settlers fresh out of the Indian wars had ill feelings about natives and their way of life. Only natives who fought back received a reservation. The Americans' appetite for land pushed natives onto reservations without respect to their tribal affiliation; many unrecognized tribes were left to fend for themselves. Some tribes today still fight for recognition from the United States Government.

Then, as American culture developed and the religious faction entered the equation, natives had to change their beliefs and traditions. The local natives lost their potlatch ceremony, which had been their history link:

> For the peoples of the Northwest Coast the potlatch is a spiritual, economic, social, legal and educational institution. They are given for special occasions. The host provides a large feast; there is singing, dancing, story-telling, speeches and then the host gives gifts. The gift-giving often occurred in order of rank and the value of the gifts corresponded to the rank of the person it was for. The leaders would also be responsible for keeping a surplus of necessities to redistribute to those in want. The potlatch was a legal and educational system in that it was the place where ownership of any properties was

told in the family histories and either verified or contested after the story-telling and speeches. (University of Victoria, "The Six Nations")

When the church complained that they were using captured slaves as gifts in the ceremonies, the United States Government outlawed the native potlatch. The Canadian Government also officially outlawed the native potlatch ceremony, but the natives practiced it anyway. Canadians were more tolerant of the natives' way of life than Americans. As a result, the First Nations Peoples, living in Canada, preserved much of their early history.

On the anniversary of Captain Cook's 1778 landing on Vancouver Island, the Canadians were celebrating his arrival as the first European in British Columbia. Four years before, in 1774, there had been a Spanish voyage by Juan Perez Hernandez; he had anchored off Nootka Sound, but he did not land. Then came a rebuttal from the First Nations Peoples of eastern Vancouver Island.

Natives of British Columbia who live on the eastern side of Vancouver Island are known as "Sne-ny-mo," meaning "people of many names," referring to a confederation that various villages formed for their better protection. From this Island Halkomelen word comes the name Nanaimo, now a city on the eastern side of Vancouver Island overlooking the Gulf of Georgia or the Georgia Strait. The Nanaimo native elders disagree that Captain Cook was the first white man to land in their country, because their oral history claims that white visitors predated the arrival of both Spanish and British explorers by many generations.

Two hundred years before the landing of Captain Cook, Francis Drake, on his journey south through the Inside Passage, sailed by the Nanaimo native villages in 1579, on route to his Birch Bay landing. Today, the city of Nanaimo is roughly 50 miles northwest of Drake's "conuenient and fit harborough". No doubt natives on both sides of the Gulf of Georgia witnessed Drake's ships on route and word spread like wildfire, in a chain reaction, throughout the whole country. But contact did not happen when Drake's ships passed these tribes in the western gulf, although it would happen later, covered in the next chapter, "The Castaways." The Nanaimo native elders over the centuries through their potlatch ceremony preserved the memory of the arrival of white visitors in today's North Puget Sound. And like Drake, not knowing how to distinguish one tribe from the other in Nova Albion, the natives likewise had no idea the white visitors were British, only that they preceded Captain Cook by many generations.

Also lost in the fold of history is the crew Drake left behind in Lummi territory, in Drake's Bay. What happened to these castaways, who were left half a world away from home and never rescued?

7

The Castaways

Mrs. Nuttall toiled through old English records to gain the number of crew members on Drake's famous voyage. She claimed he left 21 men and 1 woman behind in Nova Albion. The number of castaways would be much higher if the total number of blacks he freed was known. The number used here is around ten blacks. That brings the total castaway count to over 30.

While in the southern seas, Drake freed black men from Spanish ships and ports. He added the maroons to his crew and would later use them to man his second ship. But once the *Pelican* sank somewhere around Birch Bay, the captured *Los Reyes* didn't have room for all the treasure, the supplies, or the extra crew. Mrs. Nuttall determined that Drake arrived back in England with only 50 men. With her count and considering the crew count of 86 taken by Spanish prisoners on board the *Pelican* suggests he left about 36 crew behind.

For the long journey back to England, Drake kept only enough crew to man the *Golden Hind* and left unneeded crew at Harris Bay, within Bellingham Bay. There they set up camp among the giant firs, next to a small crystal clear creek, named Padden Creek. Drake left the extra launch from the sinking of his flagship, along with weapons, plus needed supplies to last one year, when he promised to return.

His new country supplied all the needs of man; the campers always had fresh food, like deer, numerous species of birds, salmon that spawn in the creeks, and even the occasional black bear that came to feed on fish. The native Nooksack tribe, upriver from the Lummi tribe, used Drake's Bay to dig clams. The whole area around the bay provided rich seafood, easy to catch, like Dungeness crab, lingcod, sole, and flounder.

The campsite where Drake left the castaways is located in Old

Fairhaven, a suburb of city of Bellingham. The location is down the hill toward the west end of Harris Avenue, next to where Padden creek runs into Bellingham Bay. Local natives on stormy days used Harris Bay as a campsite to escape the howling winds from the southeast, where whitecaps rolled up the channel directly into Drake's Bay. So Harris Bay supplied a well-protected location, with ample food and a suitable campsite, except for the never-ending rain, both in the summer and even heavier in the winter.

The Promise

On the long voyage home, Drake crossed the Pacific to the Spice Islands and around the Cape of Good Hope back to England. With his dream fulfilled, he became a rich man, and Queen Elizabeth I, for his contribution to the country's empty coffers, knighted him. Even after all his fame and his appointment as Mayor of Plymouth, he wasted no time in putting a return voyage together. After all, he had promised his crew in Nova Albion that he would return in one year. But as before, he needed investors. Everyone of prominence in England knew of his success, although they had no idea the plunder he brought home. The Queen kept that a secret. Drake's grand plan this time would follow the African coast south back around the Cape of Good Hope into the Pacific. He told investors that he could double their money in just one year. This left investors wondering how he could possibly achieve that; was he going back to rob the Spanish again? Drake did have a way of meeting the commitment, but he kept that to himself. Then, all of Drake's efforts and grand plans came to an end; everything stopped. Rumors claim the Queen stepped in and told Drake he could not make the voyage. The Queen grounded England's notorious privateer.

Back in Nova Albion, the now castaways waited the year and then another, and another, until they knew something had happened. There would be no return voyage.

Through all my research, every story, and local accounts, any trace of Drake's castaways in Puget Sound history hit a dead end. Then what came to mind is that this inland sea is completely isolated, and the marooned crew did not stay in the area. The circle needed to be widened. To hail a ship, their only hope, needed a view of the open Pacific, a place where they could station a lookout and ready a signal fire.

With the launch that Drake left with his crew, they explored the Strait of Juan de Fuca out to the open Pacific, but found the rocky shoreline north and south unacceptable. Any passing ships would stay far off the dangerous coast. Today, the west side of Vancouver Island is known as the graveyard of the Pacific, where fast-moving storms blow unsuspecting ships onto protruding rocks.

The marooned crew finally made a decision as to where their best chance of rescue could come from, but the launch didn't have room for everyone, so the men split up. The blacks stayed together and decided to take a land route to find the Atlantic Ocean, where they knew there would be passing ships. And the Atlantic had to be just over the mountains to the east—as slaves, they had crossed the mountains of Middle America to the Pacific, so the Atlantic couldn't be that far away.

The white members of Drake's crew, seamen and soldiers, would head north in the launch to a known island with a great view of the Pacific that Drake's ships passed on their journey south from Alaska.

The Maroons Head East

While in Nova Albion the now freed black members of Drake's crew observed that the local natives practiced slavery, both men and women they captured from enemy tribes. The blacks wanted nothing to do with the local natives or their way of life. How long they stayed in Drake's Bay is unknown; a guess would be three to five years. Their journey east to find the Atlantic would take much longer and would not go unnoticed. The natives of the country did document their presence in their oral histories.

From Drake's Bay east, the Cascade Mountains are impossible to cross; no native trails existed and all game trails came to a dead end. The first gold prospectors to the area hired the native Nooksacks to paddle them up the winding Nooksack River, where they discovered three different forks fed by the North Cascade Mountains. Prospectors who tried the overland route through the foothills to the east came back stung by nettles and bramble bushes. No prospectors ever tried that route again. But the maroons found a trail.

They followed a Lummi trade route north and then east into the Frazer Valley, in Canada. This is the home of the Sto:lo people. At Hope, British Columbia, the trail splits, one headed north and the other headed southeast through a pass in the Cascade Mountains to Okanagan country. They took the southeast trail. Following the rising sun, this trail through the pass turned back north through the mountains to Princeton, British Columbia, home of the Similkameen people. Drake's black travelers passed from the temperate rain forests of the Puget Sound to a dry climate with weather extremes, hot, cold, and windy, on the eastern slopes of the rugged Cascades.

The history of the Similkameen people can be traced back 7500 years. For centuries, these natives traded with tribes on both sides of the Cascades. They owned something everyone wanted. Tribes from as far away as the Oregon coast came to barter buffalo hides and eagle feathers; in return, they received chert and sacred ochre.

Following well-traveled native trails, the blacks headed south back into Washington State, along the eastern watershed of the Cascades, fording streams and rivers. They followed the western banks and deep basalt gorges along the wide Columbia River, as far as Vantage, Washington, where with the hot summers and low water, they crossed the mighty Columbia River.

Once on the east side of the Columbia, the country changed to sagebrush, where the winds blow most of the time and large dust devils swirl around the landscape. The climate is harsh; in the summer temperatures can reach over 100°F, and the winters are prone to freezing ground blizzards.

On this journey they passed through folded uplifted land that was once a seashore until a powerful force from the west pushed up the Cascade Mountains and filled the basin of eastern Washington with lava. They also passed through the site of the megafloods of Glacial Lake Missoula, during the last ice age. The power of rushing water and ice tore the landscape apart when an ice dam broke on the Clark Fork River at Missoula, Montana. This allowed an 800-mile-long lake to flash flood all the way to the Willamette Valley in Oregon. Large out-of-place boulders litter the land, with deep potholes carved in the earth. These megafloods are estimated to have happened at least 32 times 20,000 years ago.

Natives who lived in the country carved petroglyphs on large boulders and cliff faces on their trade routes throughout eastern Washington. Drake's black castaways followed these trails and landmarks all the way to Spokane country, where they expected to find the Atlantic Ocean. Instead, in the distance they spotted another mountain range, the Rocky Mountains. Part of the group did not want to tackle the lofty terrain, so they again split up. One group stayed near the present-day City of Spokane. The other group headed east toward Coeur d'Alene, Idaho. The black members of Drake's crew had embarked on a long journey, from the land of the Coast Salish to an endless country without a sign of the Atlantic Ocean.

One group of blacks that headed east to Coeur d'Alene country entered the land of the Interior Salish People. Legends of these people identify Drake's castaways. Native Americans pass history down by storytelling, and one native story passed down in Coeur d'Alene country is clearly not a traditional type of native story; it speaks of blacks, the "Giants and Tree Men":

> Giants were formerly common in Coeur d'Alene country. They had a very strong odor, like the odor of burning horn. Their faces were black—some say they were painted black, and the giants were taller than the highest tepees. When they saw a single tepee or lodge in a place, they would crawl up to it, rise, and look down the smoke hole. If several lodges were together, the giants were not so bold.

> Most of them dressed in bearskins, but some wore other kinds of skins with the hair left on. They lived in caves in the rocks. They had a great liking for fish, and often stole fish out of people's traps. Otherwise, they did not bother people much. They are said to have stolen women occasionally in other tribes, but there is no tradition of their having stolen women in the Coeur d'Alene country.

Other supernatural beings that used to be seen in the Coeur d'Alene and Spokane countries were called the Tree Men. They too had a strong odor. They dressed in buffalo skins and had the power to transform themselves into trees and bushes. Once, when a number of people were dancing in the Spokane country near a small lake close to the present day Cheney, they suddenly smelled a bad odor. One of them exclaimed, "That is the Tree Men!"

The people looked around and saw four men standing a little apart from one another and wearing around their shoulders buffalo skins, with the hair side out. As soon as they saw the people looking at them, they disappeared. Four bushes stood where the four Tree Men stood. (Rennard, "Giants and Tree Men")

From the Interior Salish legend, there were two different groups encountered, one in Spokane country and the other in Coeur d'Alene country. The maroons had the ability to kill large animals like bear and buffalo, but didn't know how to cure the hides. The smells the natives recognized as "Giants and Tree Men" came from trying to dry green hides over a campfire, thus the smell of burnt horn. They wore the uncured hides next to their warm bodies, hair side out, that made the smell even worse. The "Giants" had black faces because they were black men. They were tall, handpicked Spanish slaves selected for strength and their ability to do heavy work, whereas the Interior Salish people or Salish as a whole are not tall people. And tepees then were nothing like the pictures seen today of those of the Plains Indians. Interior Salish tepees, like Coast Salish, were "built close to the earth and very warm," only they used different materials, stretched animal skins sewn together. So the "Giants," or Drake's tall black castaways, could easily look down the smoke hole.

The Interior Salish had a social order that helped them survive the harsh winters, collecting wood, drying fish, sewing warm clothes. Drake's maroons feared contact with natives because they had witnessed their practice of slavery in Nova Albion. They stole fish from native traps, because they knew nothing about storing winter provisions. As a consequence, Drake's unprepared maroons, living in caves, would have eventually faded into the history of the time. Only the story of the "Giants and Tree Men" with black faces survives as a clue to what happened to part of Francis Drake's castaways.

The Voyage North

Before leaving their campsite on Padden Creek, the white seamen and soldiers of Drake's castaways likely left their own monument, or some noticeable landmark to indicate where they were heading. If a rescue ship did come for them, then the landmark would be clear and identifiable. If they carved a message on a large tree around the campsite, then it's gone, but if they chiseled their message on a large boulder or cliff face, it may still be visible somewhere in the area around Padden Creek.

Once the seamen broke camp at Harris Bay, below the present-day suburb of Old Fairhaven, and the split with the blacks occurred, the white men headed north. They passed through the territory of the Lummi tribe and then the domain of the Semiahmoo tribe, on into the western Gulf of Georgia. Along this route they traveled from island to island, depending on tides and weather conditions. Captain Vancouver noted in his journal that at times there were gale-force winds and downpours of rain. The route the castaways took was also noted by Vancouver as an inhospitable place. On their journey they definitely came in contact with other native tribes within the western boundaries of the Gulf of Georgia.

One tribe or a confederation of tribes documented this contact in their oral history. They are the Nanaimo native elders, whose ancestors witnessed or greeted the travelers on their layover. North of Nanaimo and after 138 miles up the Gulf of Georgia, they entered Discovery Pass, named for Captain Vancouver's ship, and then headed north up into the Johnstone Strait, named for James Johnstone, one of Vancouver's survey crew, who followed this waterway all the way to the open Pacific. Island jumping and living off the land, the travelers followed the eastern side of Vancouver Island to Queen Charlotte Sound. There they turned east and followed the coastline through the Inside Passage north into the Hecate Strait, where they changed course and sailed west. Their destination, the Queen Charlotte Islands, or Haida Gwaii.

Haida Gwaii is an archipelago of over 150 islands off the west coast of British Columbia, Canada. The island that Drake's seamen recalled as the best location for rescue, with a great view of the Pacific, is the most northerly island of this archipelago, Langara Island, at Dixon Entrance. Drake's ships had passed near this island on the journey south from the Gulf of Alaska, and the castaways knew this island held their best chance for hailing a ship.

The only possible rescue ships available to Drake's men were Chinese junks, although these claims are disputed. The Chinese claim to have sailed to America from 1421 on; they called the land Fu Sang. To confirm this, many artifacts have been found on the bottom of the Strait of Juan de Fuca and on the beaches of California. The Asian artifacts found date back to the 1400's and are consistent with Chinese, Japanese, or Korean cultures.

When the first Europeans made contact, natives on Haida Gwaii showed the influence of these ancient Chinese mariners. Besides being tall and white, the Haida displayed long chin beards and wore their hair in a bun atop their heads, like the Chinese.

By the time Drake's seamen made their way to Langara Island, any Chinese junks had moved their exploration down the coast to California. As it turned out, no ships sailed past Langara Island and the castaways lost all hope of rescue.

The land Drake's desperate and betrayed seamen entered, Haida Gwaii, is a rain forest environment. The rivers support salmon runs and pods of orca hunt the Inside Passage, putting on a show that can be seen and heard for miles. Haida art represents the land and animals of Haida Gwaii, carved in large totem poles. These natives built oceangoing craft with brightly colored paint that displayed distinct artistic designs.

The Haida were fearless worriers; in their oceangoing craft they traveled hundreds of miles, like the Vikings, to pillage and plunder. All of the southern tribes, even in Drake's Nova Albion, fled when they arrived. It took a British warship that bombarded their villages to put a stop to their raids south. The route Drake's seamen traveled north followed the same route the Haida had used on their southern raids for centuries.

Drake's marooned seamen blended into Haida Gwaii; years passed, and no rescue ships sailed near Langara Island. The stranded men gambled on their best location for rescue and their bet didn't pay off. The white seamen took wives and lived out the remainder of their lives among these northern natives.

The Santiago Arrives

Descendants of Drake's marooned seamen paddled out to meet the Spanish. Drake's abandoned crew had picked the best location for hailing a ship, only the meeting took place 200 years too late. In July of 1774, Juan Perez Hernandez in the *Santiago* drifted past the northwest tip of Langara Island, at Dixon Entrance. Credit is given to Juan Perez for first European contact made with the native people of British Columbia, Canada. But not so fast: Who were the light-haired, blue-eyed Haida that paddled out to meet the *Santiago*? They were English-Haida descendants, called Metis, from Francis Drake's forgotten crew.

Father Juan Crespi and Farther Tomas de la Pema y Saravia, Franciscan priests, documented the event with the Haida. The Metis wore iron or copper rings; they had iron knives and an iron boarding poke. Later, in 1792, a fur trader named Sigismund Bacstrom also confirmed the presence of blue-eyed Haida near Langara Island.

This event confused the Spaniards. They knew there had been foreign contact, but with whom? They did know the Russians were farther north in the Pacific, so they thought the Metis must have been of Russian descent. When this Spanish report came to light, descendants of Drake's settlement in Nova Albion were put into the equation, but discounted, because it was too far north for Drake to have sailed. Still, there they were.

The blue-eyed, light-haired Metis of Haida Gwaii could not have been of Russian descent. In 1728, Russian Czar Peter the Great sent Vitus Jonassen Bering of Denmark to determine whether Asia and America were separate continents. By 1741, the Russians had reached 55° north, the lower panhandle of Alaska, but had not established any foothold or trade in Haida Gwaii, at 54° 30 min. Thirty-three years later, in 1774, Juan Perez showed up in the *Santiago*, off Langara Island, and documented the Metis. Even using a 50-year window, it is impossible for the Russians to have made contact and produced full-grown blue-eyed offspring on Langara Island.

Furthermore, Russians had a bad reputation with native peoples of the north—they were brutal. Russian traders took hostages, killed a few, and forced the others to bring them sea otter pelts. The northern natives did fight back, resulting in the Russian Aleut War. Word about Russian trade practices and their brutality spread throughout the northern country, and when the Russians ventured on shore, the natives killed them.

Russian contact doesn't fit in identifying the Metis of Langara Island. Only Francis Drake's marooned seamen who left Nova Albion seeking rescue works with the light-haired, blue-eyed Metis of Haida Gwaii.

Missed by historians is that there was an attempt made in 1582 to rescue the stranded men, plus much more. Drake, grounded by the Queen, had left something else in Nova Albion, and he wanted it back. So he sent his young cousin John, then in his early twenties, to do his bidding. John was the only person Drake trusted to carry out the task, and for his loyalty, he would be well rewarded.

8

John Drake and the Fenton Expedition

In 1580, Elizabeth I had stopped Drake's return voyage to Nova Albion, but that didn't mean someone else couldn't do his bidding. In 1582, Drake found Edward Fenton, who agreed to make the voyage. As one of the investors, Drake helped organize the Fenton Expedition of three ships, and for his contribution added a small bark of 40 tons named the *Francis.* In charge of this ship, Drake assigned his young cousin John, who had helped document the famous voyage as an artist and page. John, then in his early twenties, had sailed with Drake for nine years while in training and service. Along with John in the *Francis*, Drake also supplied navigators and a few crew members who had sailed on his famous voyage. John and the navigators all knew the location of Nova Albion.

Before the Fenton Expedition sailed, word spread to Drake and some crew members that Edward Fenton had secret dealings with the Spanish ambassador. But the rumors seemed baseless, so everything went ahead as planned.

Besides Drake's *Francis* of 40 tons, the three other ships in the fleet were the *Leicester* of 400 tons, the *Edward Bonaventure* of 250 tons, and the *Elizabeth* of 50 tons. What investors loaded into these ships is not clear, but what came to light later in court cases is that they planned to set up factories and leave men behind to maintain them. Where they planned to set up the factories is not known, but with Drake organizing the expedition, where else but Nova Albion and the Spice Islands. But an interesting question here is, why did Drake send such a small ship, the smallest in the fleet? One would think the more cargo you could load into a ship, the more money you could make. This important question has an answer that will come to light later.

The Fenton Expedition sailed on May 1st, 1582; their route was top secret. The ships were well armed and had enough supplies to last two years. They sailed down the African coast to the Cape Verde Islands, where Fenton traded the 50-ton *Elizabeth* for supplies—a strange transaction, since investors had loaded enough supplies for two years. Then, instead of following the African coast south toward the Cape of Good Hope, as Drake's earlier grand plan would have followed, the smaller fleet of three turned west toward the coast of Brazil.

The trip along the route to Brazil, as it turns out, answers the supply question: With all the officers and gentlemen on board, this voyage supported one big high-society party, with all the trimmings. By the time the fleet reached the coast of Brazil, supplies were low again, mainly the wine. Once there, Fenton blamed the merchants for not giving them enough supplies to last two years.

While deciding what to do next, Fenton spotted a Spanish ship and sent John Drake in the *Francis* to chase it down. On board the ship they happened upon an Englishman named Richard Carter, who had lived in Argentina for 20 years. There, the Spaniards called him Juan Perez. While detained from his business trip to Brazil, Richard Carter had a conversation with John Drake about Francis Drake's famous voyage around the world. No doubt John carried on, because he liked to brag, something he had picked up from his noted mentor.

Then Fenton sent for Carter, wanting to know the whereabouts of the Spanish fleet and where more wine and supplies could be purchased. Carter told Fenton that the Spanish fleet had departed the Strait of Magellan six weeks before and that supplies could be obtained, but the wine he sought would take three months. With this news, Fenton released Carter to go about his business. Fenton then called all the officers and gentlemen together for a council.

In the meeting the majority decided that the voyage could not continue without the needed supplies and that they would return to England. John Drake did not accept the council's decision; he returned to the *Francis* and deserted to continue the voyage on his own. At this point, Fenton headed up the coast of Brazil toward the Caribbean, and John Drake headed down the Brazilian coast following the same route as Drake's famous voyage.

Fenton's two ships, the *Leicester* and the *Edward Bonaventure*, encountered the Spanish fleet at the harbor of Saint Vincent in the Caribbean. A battle ensued and the Englishmen fought for their lives to escape, taking casualties. William Hawkins, a cousin of Francis Drake, was killed in this encounter. Battered and lucky to be afloat, the Fenton Expedition limped back to England.

Merchants and investors, including Francis Drake, lost all their investments. In court cases that followed, changes were made to the way future enterprises in England were financed. The Fenton Expedition turned out to be a complete failure, with the loss of lives and a heavy financial cost to all. But more important, what happened to John Drake in the *Francis*, and why did he desert Fenton?

John Drake, now on his own in the *Francis* with a crew of 17, headed down the coast of Brazil on route for the Strait of Magellan. They too ran short of supplies and went exploring up a large river, the Rio de la Plata or the Silver River, between Uruguay and Argentina. There, the *Francis* hit submerged rocks and sank, leaving all aboard to fend for themselves. Once on shore, John wandered around in the strange country until finally making his way to Buenos Aires, Argentina, where he mixed with the local residents. Then he made a big mistake: he started to brag and play the big shot, relating how he had sailed with Francis Drake. Well, people took note. Even in Argentina everyone knew of "the dragon" and Drake's exploits in the Pacific. This alerted Spanish authorities, who let the locals entertain John until they could check out his story.

Spanish authorities sent for Juan Perez, the Englishman known as Richard Carter, who had just returned from his business trip to Brazil. Carter identified John as the one who had detained his ship while with the Fenton Expedition off the coast of Brazil. Carter also told Spanish authorities that John had boasted to him that he had sailed with Francis Drake in the Pacific. With John's story confirmed, authorities took him into custody.

John knew from family stories what happened to Englishmen who trespassed in Spanish territory. He knew about the Hawkins fleet and the slaughter of Englishmen at San Juan de Ulúa. Scared and willing to do just about anything, but not everything, to save his life, John switched religions. He took the Catholic oath and his first deposition to Spanish authorities took place in Santa Fe, Argentina. In his first deposition, H. R. Wagner stated, "John even had the hardihood to say Francis Drake repaired his ship at a bay in 48°." John told the truth in this first deposition, but in a second deposition later the N 48° will become part of a Spanish cover-up. Holding back, John never did reveal what he was going to do with one small ship.

About four years after John's first deposition, Spain ordered him off on a long journey across the continent to Lima, Peru. In Callao, Port of Lima, on the famous voyage years earlier, Drake had entered the harbor at night searching for ships loaded with silver, but all of the ships had been empty. So he had cut their anchor cables and commandeered and looted the ship of Alonsó Rodriguez Bautista, which had just entered the harbor. Unlike Santa Fe, where John made his first deposition, Lima had Spanish navigators for the Pacific, and they knew the winds and currents as far north as California. In Lima, John made his second deposition, but before that happened, he faced the brutality of Spanish interrogators.

In his second deposition, according to Spain, John was now a good Catholic. But he answered only the questions interrogators gave him permission to answer. He had a show trial. What Spanish navigators gleaned from John Drake never saw the light of day; Spain kept those records in secret archives. Mrs. Nuttall confirmed the secret archives in *New Light on Drake*, when she tried to research Nuña da Silva, the Portuguese pilot and shipowner Drake had captured off the Cape Verde Islands and then released in lower Mexico. Mrs. Nuttall stated, "the fact that the main part of the proceso against da Silva was kept in the secret archives of the inquisition accounts for its destruction."

But were these archives really destroyed? No—they were shipped back to Spain and used later to compile a story about a voyage to the Pacific Northwest by Admiral de Fonté. De Fonté and Juan de Fuca will be covered later.

Spain knew in 1587, from John Drake, that Francis Drake had landed in a bay at N 48°. They also knew, from John, the name of the Spanish ship, the *Los Reyes*, Francis Drake commandeered and took to the Pacific Northwest. The following is John's statement about Drake's Nova Albion:

> Francis Drake, on this journey, saw five or six islands of
> good land. He called one San Bartolome, one San Jaime,

and another which seemed to be the largest and best, Nueva Albion. Here he remained a month and a half, repairing the two ships which he had with him (Wagner, *Sir Francis Drake's Voyage*).

From John's statement, he "saw five or six islands of good land," the important words here are *good land*; that means there was unsuitable land also, or more than five or six islands. Between the San Juan group and the Gulf Islands of British Columbia, there are over 400 islands ranging in size from high-standing mountains to big flat rocks; today, most of these islands are not settled.

Next, John gave the name *San Bartolome*; what he meant is Saint Bartholomew, where thousands of French Protestants were killed in Catholic mob violence. Francis Drake had first learned about this incident while in the Caribbean from French Captain Tetû, before the two intercepted the Spanish silver train. Francis Fletcher, the ship's pastor, had preached about this religious massacre on the famous voyage.

So John used this name to send a message that Spanish interrogators threatened his life if he didn't reveal Drake's North American landing site. Still, he never gave away Drake's real landing spot. He never said they landed on the mainland, and he only gave Spanish interrogators the N 48°, which they presumed to be on the Pacific Coast, but that is over 100 miles away from Drake's Bay.

Still deceptive about Drake's real landing site, John said they named "one San Jaime, and another which seemed to be the largest and best, Nueva Albion." Drake named all the islands in the North Puget Sound as the Islands of Saint James, and as for the largest and best, that is Vancouver Island. The only way John would have known that Vancouver Island was an island and not a part of the mainland is that Drake had sailed down the Inside Passage between Vancouver Island and the mainland of British Columbia, on a southeast route from Queen Charlotte Sound.

Under threat of death, John was questioned by Spanish interrogators about Drake's ship and the ships he captured. They surely asked, What was the name of the ship? Where did he capture the ship? What did he do with the ship? John got caught up in question after question and revealed that Drake had kept the *Los Reyes*. And as per John's statement about

Drake's two ships, the *Los Reyes* was Drake's second ship in Nova Albion.

Spanish interrogators were ruthless. They beat and tortured their prisoners to get answers. Even though John had converted to Catholicism, that meant nothing; being an Englishman and related to their archenemy the dragon meant death. If released, John would inform Francis Drake that he had revealed the N 48°, and Spain needed to keep that secret for a good reason. They kept Francis Drake under surveillance, and if he headed back to the Pacific, they would know where to engage him.

So once interrogators drained John of all usable information, they executed him. Spain did the same to John Oxenham, another Englishman and one of Drake's friends captured on the coast of the Pacific. Local authorities received the execution orders from the top of the Spanish Government, and their orders stated, "sink every English ship and kill every Englishman." After John Drake's second deposition in Lima, Peru, *no* one ever heard from him again.

John's Mission with Fenton

Unknown to Edward Fenton, John had important business to conduct for Francis Drake. That is why he deserted the Fenton Expedition when the council decided to return to England. Spanish interrogators never did find out what John planned to do with one small ship, the *Francis* of 40 tons. The next question to ask here is, why did Francis Drake send the smallest ship in the Fenton Expedition? If he planned to make a lot of money from setting up factories and transporting goods back to England, then a larger ship seems reasonable. No, he needed the small ship in Nova Albion, to sail back through his Islands of Saint James, or today's San Juan Islands.

In 1579, Francis Drake left men behind in Nova Albion, but still that wasn't the driving force behind John Drake's need to continue the voyage on his own. His real motive was money. In his mind, he was going to become a rich man. All he had to do was retrieve what Drake left behind in Nova Albion. To understand why Drake needed money, one has to look back to after he returned home and the Queen knighted him. The Queen rewarded him and his investors well, but Drake didn't know how to handle the wealth. With gold and silver bars, he bought expensive property and tried to buy his way into high society by giving silver bars away to important gentlemen. His fortune began to dwindle fast and he needed more. But what grand plan did he have this time, and where would more gold and silver come from?

The Queen stopped Sir Francis from his grand plan to sail back to the Pacific in 1580. At the time, while trying to put a return voyage together, he offered investors double their investment in just one year. If he wasn't going back to rob the Spanish again, who were on guard and keeping track of him, then the only answer is that he had left a fortune behind in Nova Albion.

John Drake agreed to retrieve the hidden fortune, of which he would receive a good share. He had a plan with the Fenton Expedition once they reached Nova Albion. He would leave Fenton with his large ships next to one of the islands, "the largest and best," Vancouver Island. Then once Fenton determined where to construct a factory site, John would continue on into today's Strait of Juan de Fuca, to Drake's hidden bay, Bellingham Bay. He would pick up Drake's marooned men and Drake's hidden booty and then continue on to the Spice Islands and home.

It was a simple plan that could have worked if Drake had chosen someone other than Edward Fenton. Then John Drake would never have deserted and sailed up the Silver River where the *Francis* hit submerged rocks and sank. And Spanish interrogators, through their torture, would never have attained the location of Drake's North American landing site. As it turned out, John wasn't honest with Spanish navigators, and they would find that out when they sent pilot Juan the Greek north to locate Drake's Bay.

9

The Spanish Sail North

The Voyages of Fuca and De Fonté

After the 1587 interrogation of John Drake in Lima, Peru, Spain thought they knew where Francis Drake had landed on the northwest coast of America. Although Spain claimed the whole Pacific Ocean, often called *the Spanish Lake,* they had never sailed to N 48° or anywhere in the North Pacific. With permission from the Viceroy, a fleet of three small ships, with Juan the Greek as navigator, headed north to find Drake's harbor. Because the cold California current runs south along the coast from the northern waters, the fleet needed to sail out to sea and then back in at the selected degrees. But something happened on Spain's first voyage north and a mutiny broke out. Rumor had it that crimes of the captain were to blame. Unable to continue, the fleet sailed back to New Spain.

Then in the same year, 1587, all planned voyages were put on hold: Spain had another intruder in the Pacific, English buccaneer Thomas Cavendish. He followed the same route around the bottom of South America as Drake and caught the Spanish off guard again, escaping with Spanish gold. Then came the 1588 war with England, where the Spanish Armada met a crushing defeat, which Francis Drake took part in. Drake's involvement against the armada will be covered later. Now with slim resources, Spain needed to approve every voyage, even in the Pacific, with cost in mind.

In 1592, five years after the first attempt, Spain sent another voyage north to find Drake's harbor. Only this time they sent Juan the Greek with one small ship and a pinnace. Most historians believe Juan's voyage never happened, because all the information came from a second-hand source, an English mapmaker named Michael Loc. But the Greek's voyage did happen; the problem is that Loc misunderstood what the old Greek navigator told him and the information directed historians down a dead-end road.

Michael Loc claimed to have met with the Greek navigator in Italy, in 1596. The Greek's real name was Apostolos Valerianos; he had served the Spanish Government in the Pacific for 40 years. In the conversation between the Englishman and the Greek, they spoke in Italian and Spanish—a dilemma that we should explore before we get into what the two spoke about. Greek is the hardest language for an Englishman to understand, because of the vowels, and it doesn't matter which language the two spoke in—the Greek accent always comes through when vowels are spoken. In Greek, the ancestor of the letter Y is the Semitic letter "waw," from which come F, U, and W. Here we are speaking about old Greek, because languages change over the centuries. Juan the Greek had trouble pronouncing the U, because it is derived from the same place as the F, so when he tried to pronounce a word that started with the letter U, the F sound came through.

Michael Loc, in his conversation with the old Greek navigator, thought Juan called himself, while working for Spain, Juan de Fuca. Wrong. And this is where the misunderstanding happened. The Greek really stated to Loc the name of the river or strait he discovered within N 48° and charted as Juan de Ulua, short for San Juan de Ulua. Juan had charted this name because his mission was to search for Drake's harbor, and this name connects directly to a battle in 1568 where Spain claimed a great victory over John Hawkins and Francis Drake.

Most Spanish seamen heading for the Pacific came through San Juan de Ulua (*Ulca*), the harbor of Veracruz, but when they spoke about how they arrived, they used the shorter version of the name, Juan de Ulua.

No Spanish navigator by the name of Juan de Fuca has ever been documented in Spanish history. Englishman Michael Loc's misnomer in translation while speaking to the Greek navigator started historians on this fictional path. Thus, historians determined that the voyage of Juan the Greek to the Pacific Northwest never happened. No charts or documents about Spain's voyage north to N 48° in 1592 has ever been located, but there is an account of another, later Spanish voyage that connects directly to the Greek's 1592 voyage.

Admiral De Fonté

Spain cooked up the voyage of Admiral de Fonté in 1640. They claimed he sailed from Lima, Peru, and found the Northwest Passage at N 53°. But to fabricate the de Fonté voyage, Spain needed something to work from, so they used the charts and logs from 1592 made by Juan the Greek. Spain in the 1600's still possessed Juan's account in their secret archives. Mrs. Nuttall confirmed the secret archives in *New Light on Drake*. But she thought Spain had destroyed all the old accounts. Wrong again. The logs and charts of the Greek's voyage had ended up in Spain.

Spain composed a letter that claimed territory to N 53°. A dead giveaway that Spain used the logs and charts of Juan the Greek from 1592 to construct the voyage of Admiral de Fonté in 1640 comes in the description of the route the Admiral took. Henry Hudson had discovered Hudson Bay in 1610, but no one at that time knew the breadth of the North American continent. The Admiral de Fonté letter, where the fictional voyage originated, claims to have sent an expedition from the Pacific Northwest overland to Hudson Bay. This was first published in England, in *Memoirs for the Curious*, in 1708. How the de Fonté story connects to Juan the Greek is found in this statement, in the first part of his account. From the de Fonté story, "they sailed north, then northeast into a large lake, where they saw islands and a peninsula. They saw natives in canoes fifty feet long and the natives had Salmon and other types of fish." (Drage, *The Great Probability of a Northwest Passage*)

From the Michael Loc story, Juan the Greek said he had sailed for 20 days and claimed to have found the Northwest Passage, but Spain did not pay him for his discoveries, so he wanted to work for the Queen to find a new route to the Pacific if she would supply two ships.

In 1592, Juan the Greek did explore for 20 days, and in doing so he charted the western side of Vancouver Island in search of Drake's harbor. But to find out what the Greek charted, one has to read the first

Map of the fabricated Spanish voyage of Admiral de Fonté.

The Library of Congress. Licensed under Public domain via Wikimedia Commons.

part of the Admiral de Fonté story from 1640. At the southeast tip of Vancouver Island, Juan sailed "north" into today's Haro Strait, then he sailed "northeast" through today's Boundary Pass and then into a "large lake," today's lower Gulf of Georgia. This matches the de Fonté passage above. On his course he saw natives in canoes 50 feet long with salmon and other types of fish. This description of natives and fish is why the Greek thought he was in a large river and a large lake, because salmon during their life cycle return to fresh water. The Greek encountered the Coast Salish from the Saanich Peninsula, who fished these waters. They are the Tsartlip, Tsawout, Pauquachin, and Tseycum. Another tribe in the same location were on San Juan Island, facing the Haro Strait; they were the Songlish/Lummi. Millions of salmon stream through this waterway in the summer heading for the Frazer River in Canada.

Juan, once in the large lake, or the lower Gulf of Georgia, saw "islands"; they are to the northwest, the Gulf Islands of British Columbia, and to the south, the San Juan Islands. From his location, looking north, he spotted a "peninsula," today's Point Roberts. Juan never sailed any farther; at that point he turned back. But from where he stopped, he had a view of upper Boundary Bay on the east side of the Peninsula. The upper bay, about 15 miles away, appears to run north as far as the eye can see. Northern Boundary Bay is what Juan perceived to be the Northwest Passage. Juan the Greek, in 1592, unknowingly had discovered the North Puget Sound. From where the Greek navigator turned back, Spain fabricated the rest of the de Fonté story, which claimed to go overland to Hudson Bay. Spain leaked this Admiral de Fonté letter to the French; from there, it made its way to England and was published in 1708.

Why did Spain use the discoveries of Juan the Greek for the voyage of Admiral de Fonté? At the time, just sailing to a location was enough to lay claim to the country. In England, Elizabeth I had passed away and accounts of Drake's famous voyage were published. Rumors were floating around the English court that Francis Drake's Nova Albion was located somewhere around N 50°. Spies passed these rumors on to Spain. So Spain, in turn, to lay claim to the country above N 50°, fabricated the voyage of Admiral de Fonté, using the information and discoveries of Juan the Greek from N 48°. Then Spain moved Juan's discoveries within N 48° to N 53° to stay one jump ahead of English claims. Nothing at N 53° matches or even comes close to what Spain described for the de Fonté voyage.

On the map of the de Fonté voyage, Spain made a mistake. They didn't have enough information from Juan's charts, so they put the "islands" he observed in the wrong location. Juan saw the islands after he sailed north through today's Haro Strait, then northeast through today's Boundary Pass, into a large lake or today's lower Gulf of Georgia. Confused about the correct location, Spain drew the islands at the southwest entrance of the large river, or today's Strait of Juan de Fuca. The Spanish mapmaker thought that when Juan sail north and then northeast, he was out in the open Pacific heading for N 48°, so that is how islands appeared on the de Fonté map—where there are none, at the southwest entrance to the Strait of Juan de Fuca.

To top off the de Fonté fabrication, Spain used information from their secret archives, the interrogation of John Drake in 1587. In the archives, John disclosed the name of the ship, the *Los Reyes*, stolen by Francis Drake, his second ship in Nova Albion. So Spain named the large river, today's Strait of Juan de Fuca, *Rio de Los Reyes* (River of the *Los Reyes*). But as already stated, Spain had moved the location from within N 48° to N 53° to outdo English rumors that Drake had landed around N 50°.

The Voyage of Juan the Greek did happen in 1592, but he never found Drake's Bay. He came close, though; from where he stopped and turned back in the lower Gulf of Georgia, he could see, across the large lake to the east, Drake's "white banks and cliffs that face the sea." The charts of Juan the Greek on his 20-day exploration of the west side of Vancouver Island and into the lower Gulf of Georgia showed the layout of five major harbors. Juan's charts would later direct Juan Perez, in 1774, to Nootka Sound on the northwest side of Vancouver Island.

Voyage of the Santiago

After the voyage of Juan the Greek, about 180 years passed without European voyagers venturing to the Pacific Northwest. Then Spain received information that the Russians were moving into the North Pacific. Because Spain claimed the whole Pacific Ocean, they wanted to know whether the Russians were trespassing in their territory. In 1774, Spain sent the sloop of war, *Santiago*, north to look for Russian settlements. On this voyage, Juan Perez Hernandez sailed to N 54° 40 min, but he didn't get close enough to shore to see much, nor did he send anyone ashore to claim any land. The *Santiago* did drift by Langara Island at the northern end of the Queen Charlotte Islands, at Dixon Entrance, where natives rowed out to trade.

Here two Franciscan priests documented the light-haired, blue-eyed, "Metis" of Haida Gwaii. This first Spanish contact with the Haida, roughly 200 years after Drake's marooned crew landed there, is said to have started the smallpox epidemic. The high native death toll in Haida Gwaii reduced the native population of thousands to about 900 souls. Along with the high death toll went much of the Haida's oral history that likely, through their stories, went back to their arrival on the Islands thousands of years before.

On the Spaniards' voyage back south in the *Santiago*, they anchored off Nootka Sound on the northwest side of Vancouver Island, but no one landed. But natives did paddle out to trade. Juan Perez knew the location of Nootka Sound because he had the charts of Juan the Greek from 1592. On his 20-day exploration, the Greek, using a pinnace, charted five major harbors on the west side of Vancouver Island while hunting for Drake's harbor, within N 48°, as revealed by John Drake.

Later, when the Spaniards were asked if they had seen a strait to the east at N 48°, Esteban Jose Martinez, second in command of the *Santiago*, claimed they did see the strait. Untrue; no one on the *Santiago* saw any strait to the east. Where Martinez had seen the strait at N 48° was on the 1592 charts of Juan the Greek. Here is the proof: Nootka Sound, where the *Santiago* anchored, is on the northwest side of Vancouver Island. That is 100 miles away—too far away to see the strait—plus the Greek thought the strait was a large river. At the same time, the Spaniards on the *Santiago* were all sick from scurvy, and they lost their anchor off Nootka Sound, so they set a fast course back to Mexico. On this fast course, Juan Perez headed out to sea, on a southwest line, and did not sail southeast down the dangerous rocky coastline of Vancouver Island to observe the strait. But they knew the strait or the large river was there, just like they knew Nootka Sound was there, because they carried the charts of Juan the Greek.

On a follow-up voyage in 1775, Spanish explorers Bruno de Heceta and Bodega y Quadra sailed to Washington State and British Columbia, charting and claiming land, but these Spanish seamen were out of their element. The weather in the Pacific Northwest most of the time is wet, and the sea is cold. Their biscuits molded and their dress was inadequate. Unlike British seamen, who had a good diet on long voyages, Spanish explorers were 200 years behind in combating scurvy. The treatment of the day for the sick and weakened seamen was bloodletting, a deadly cure, and many died. On later voyages barrels of lime juice were sent north, but Spanish seamen and soldiers still got sick. Once home, the crew who had lived needed a long recovery. Scurvy wasn't the only problem; Spanish ships were floating disease factories. In an attempt to combat the problem, Spain issued orders that all bedding be brought above deck and aired out.

The Written History Begins

In the late 1700's, the written history started for the Pacific Northwest. In 1513, Balboa had claimed the Pacific Ocean, as well as the adjoining lands, for the Spanish Crown. But England did not recognize these Spanish claims, because they figured that no one had the right to claim the whole western hemisphere. So in 1778, English Captain James Cook showed up in the Pacific Northwest on his third voyage of exploration, landing at Nootka Sound on the northwest side of Vancouver Island. At the time, the local natives displayed four silver spoons from the *Santiago*, acquired four years earlier. While charting his way north, Captain Cook missed the entrance to today's Strait of Juan de Fuca. Storm after storm blew him off course, and he ended up out at sea before landing at Nootka Sound. Later, when asked whether he had seen a strait to the east, he claimed it did not exist. Also, during this period both English and Spanish explorers thought Vancouver Island was the mainland. These early explorers didn't know the Puget Sound existed.

Captain Cook went on to explore and chart the North Pacific, searching for the Northwest Passage, followed by a French explorer, La Pérouse. After these two European voyages, fur traders from six different nations began to show up in Spanish-claimed territory without a license. Even the American Robert Gray, based in Boston, was on the coast flying a red, white, and blue flag no one had seen before.

Still concerned about Russians settlements, Spain sent two noteworthy navigators north again. First Jose Maria Narvaez contacted the Russians in Alaska, followed by Esteban Jose Martinez, who had a social and imbibing meeting with them. He reported that the Russians planned to construct a settlement at Nootka Sound on Vancouver Island.

Martinez, second in command of the *Santiago* in 1774, was now a sea captain. But no one wanted to sail with him—he drank too much and had fits of rage. His crew did report him for misconduct, but nothing happened, because he had connections to or was related to the Viceroy.

When Martinez showed up at Nootka Sound on May 5th, 1789, he discovered fur traders. While the Spanish were absent from the Pacific Northwest, retired Royal Navy Captain John Meares had set up a fur trading business, with a good market in China, called the Northwest America Company. To get around acquiring a Spanish license and the monopoly of the East India Company, his ships were registered as Portuguese, which didn't need a license. Captain Meares was not at Nootka Sound at the time; instead, in his place, Captain James Colnett and his Chinese crew were conducting their fur trading business.

Martinez first confronted American Robert Gray, who said he was leaving, so Martinez let him go. Captain Gray had been trading on northern Vancouver Island, when a problem occurred with the local natives. What the natives would later tell the Spanish is that Captain Gray wanted furs, and when they didn't want to trade, he loaded his cannons and blew their village to bits, then took the furs. But Captain Gray had witnessed something he didn't like, and that is why he had sent cannon volleys into the village; later, the Spanish would also witness the same thing and try to stop the practice: The northern Vancouver Island natives captured slaves, and when food was scarce, they practiced cannibalism.

Between May 5th, and July 2nd, 1789, Martinez confronted six ships; two were released, but Captain Colnett, a perky Englishman at no loss for words, irritated Martinez—a big mistake, because he ordered all English ships and one American ship confiscated.

The ships Martinez seized at Nootka Sound were the American ship *Columbia Rediviva*, with Captain John Kendrick, based in Boston. Three English ships were seized: the *Princes Royal*, the *Argonaut*, and a small prefab schooner, the *Northwest America*, 33 feet long with eight oars and a shallow draft.

In a ceremony, Martinez then reclaimed Nootka Sound and the Northwest Coast for Spain. He used Colnett's Chinese crew as slave labor to build a fort, which he named San Miguel. With building construction going on, Martinez had something else in mind; he had the small schooner *Northwest America*, which could get close to shore and search for the harbor of Francis Drake, as revealed in 1587 by John Drake.

Spain in the late 1700's possessed all the information about Drake's famous voyage that we have today, only they knew the N 48° of his landing site. So using the small schooner *Northwest America*, Martinez sent pilot and explorer Jose Maria Narvaez south along the west side of Vancouver Island to locate Drake's Bay.

The west side of Vancouver Island has five major ports indenting the rocky coastline, plus numerous small areas to search, so Narvaez headed south, entering and exploring port after port, until he had sailed about 60 miles into the 90-mile-long Strait of Juan de Fuca, around today's British Columbia capital city, Victoria. From where he stopped, the San Juan Islands to the east appeared all bunched together and looked like they were part of the mainland. So Narvaez turned back and did not locate Drake's Bay at N 48°. He didn't sail as far as Juan the Greek, who had proceeded north from the same location, up the Haro Strait, then northeast through Boundary Pass into the lower Gulf of Georgia. Once Narvaez sailed back to Nootka Sound, the only harbor he could recommend was Port Renfrew at the northern entrance to the Strait of Juan de Fuca, but that wasn't Drake's Bay.

After Narvaez returned to Nootka Sound, Martinez had the prefab schooner *Northwest America* dismantled and loaded up, then all confiscated ships and crews were taken south to San Blas, Mexico. He left Nootka Sound unattended. At San Blas, the Spanish released the American ship *Columbia Rediviva*, because the two countries were allies against the British during the American Revolution, but Spain kept all the English ships.

This Nootka Sound incident turned into an international event that almost started a war. In England, tempers flared, and Royal Navy Captain John Mears fanned the flames, even lying about his losses. As the two countries prepared for war, France stepped in to cool the situation down and bring the two parties together. This resulted in the Nootka Sound Convention, where England and Spain came to an agreement for seized English property, mainly about the ships and payment for the crews. A hang-up came in negotiations about the property at Nootka Sound that Captain John Mears claimed to have obtained from the local chief.

With the Nootka Sound Convention going on, Spain sent another fleet back north to occupy Nootka Sound in 1790, headed by Lieutenant Francisco de Eliza. Esteban Jose Martinez also accompanied the fleet, but as a non-officer. Spain had demoted him for almost starting a war.

Spain also issued orders not to bother any other fur trading vessels. In Eliza's fleet, Spain used one of the confiscated English ships, the 65-ton, sloop rigged *Princes Royal* that had belonged to the King George's Sound Company, which had merged with the Northwest America Company. Captain John Mears had gone bankrupt. But Spain still had the ship and renamed her the *Princesa Real.* They assigned Sub-Lieutenant Manuel Quimper as captain, and while in San Blas, he added more guns to the English ship, bringing the count to four cannons and eight swivel guns.

The fleet that headed back to Nootka Sound, headed by Spanish-born Francisco de Eliza, consisted of a detachment of soldiers and enough supplies to reoccupy Fort San Miguel, built by Esteban Jose Martinez one year earlier. But when they arrived, they were not welcomed; tensions with the local natives were high, because a year earlier Martinez had shot and killed their chief, Callicum, when he boarded Martinez's ship to make a complaint. So Eliza's duties began with the need to calm the fears of the local natives. Plus, the Viceroy had ordered Eliza to convert them to Catholicism.

Due to English claims in the Nootka Convention, Spain found it more important than ever to locate Drake's harbor at N 48°. If fur traders fanning out over the country found his harbor first, England could claim this whole northern country, and that would mean war. From Nootka Sound, Eliza ordered Salvador Fidalgo to explore north and Manuel Quimper to explore south. Jose Maria Narvaez, one year earlier, had checked out the harbors south along the west side of Vancouver Island and found nothing. But Manuel Quimper, using the English ship, headed back to check them again.

Voyage of the Princesa Real

Sub-Lieutenant Manual Quimper was born in Peru, of a Spanish mother and a French father, and started his navy career at the age of 13 as a cadet. Smart and willing, he received an endorsement from the Peruvian Viceroy to attend the University of San Marcos, in Lima. He majored in mathematics and nautical applications and was recognized for his cartographic skills.

Peruvians during this time were rebelling against Spanish rule. All their riches and resources ended up in Spain, and as a people, they were second-class citizens. Resentments were the fact, even in the Spanish Navy; when two officers of the same rank were in competition for a post, the one born in America became second in command. Spanish-born officers took command. There were exceptions: Bodega y Quadra, a Peruvian, became commandant of the marine department at San Blas.

Francisco de Eliza gave Quimper two months to explore south and then return to Nootka Sound by August 15th. He started in Clayoquot Sound, where he found it necessary to trade with the local natives for two canoes. The English ship he was using, the 65-ton *Princesa Real*, only had a four-oared rowboat. With the canoes, Quimper sent out two pilots, Lopes de Haro and Juan Carrasco, to thoroughly search the harbors Narvaez had entered the year before. Following Vancouver Island, which points southeast into the Strait of Juan de Fuca, they searched harbor after harbor until they came to the southeast point of the Island. This is where Jose Maria Narvaez turned back, about 60 miles into the strait. Juan Carrasco later stated that from where Quimper searched the southeast tip of Vancouver Island, the San Juan Islands farther east looked like they were part of the mainland.

From the southeast tip of Vancouver Island, Quimper decided to sail farther east to search the south side of the Strait of Juan de Fuca. On his course, still heading southeast, he spotted islands to the north, none of which he documented. From the John Drake interrogation in Lima in 1587, Quimper knew that John had revealed that "there were five or six islands of good land." This first clue prompted Quimper to start looking for a harbor where a large ship could land. On the southeast side of the Strait of Juan de Fuca, he anchored the renamed English ship in Discovery Bay. There he took readings and found it still within N 48°. From where Narvaez turned back, Manuel Quimper sailed 30 miles farther east, spotted islands, and anchored in Discovery Bay, where he sent out two scouting parties.

While in Discovery Bay, natives in canoes came to trade. Quimper had traded with different tribes along his 200-mile journey from Nootka Sound to the eastern end of the Strait of Juan de Fuca, but these natives wore coins as earrings. He wasn't clear about what kind of coins, but thought they could be English, Portuguese, or Chinese. So far, at the eastern end of the strait, he had two clues, first the islands and now contact with foreign coins. This to him confirmed that Drake's Bay must be somewhere in the area.

The Spanish Cover-Up

H. R. Wagner's book *Spanish Exploration in the Strait of Juan de Fuca* followed the journal of Manuel Quimper. But all of Quimper's papers and journals had been destroyed in a Peruvian uprising, so where did Wagner find the records? What Wagner found and followed were edited copies, which described where Quimper planted crosses and buried bottles to claim the country. Wagner even traveled to the area twice and tried to find these locations, without success. Spain fabricated these stories to add a little color to his voyage. But, even though Spain covered up Quimper's real findings, they missed several points, as did H. R. Wagner.

The first clue that Quimper discovered Drake's Bay came in the names he charted at the east end of the Strait of Juan de Fuca. From where he anchored in Discovery Bay, he claimed to have observed north across the water ten miles away, today's Rosario Strait. Historians claim Quimper thought the Rosario Strait was a bay, and he named the bay Boca de Fidalgo. "Boca" means entrance and "de" means "of," but Fidalgo has two meanings. Here, remember that Quimper had graduated from the University of San Marcos, in Lima; he was a smart fellow. Fidalgo can be a surname, and historians have assumed that Quimper named this bay after Salvador Fidalgo, who was a part of Eliza's fleet and had gone to search north of Nootka Sound. But Fidalgo can also mean an English gentleman who had inherited nobility or gained knighthood through his accomplishments while in the service of the state, like Francis Drake. Furthermore, Quimper's Boca de Fidalgo just happens to be Drake's exit route from his hidden harbor in the *Golden Hind*. So to Quimper, Boca de Fidalgo meant that this was the entrance to Drake's Bay.

From where Quimper anchored in Discovery Bay, he sent out Lopes de Haro and Juan Carrasco, one in a canoe and the other in the four-oared rowboat. He kept one canoe with the *Princesa Real*. Quimper ordered his explorers to check out two points of interest, but which two points? He did not say. Again, judging from the names Quimper assigned, the two explorers headed north from Discovery Bay and either passed a dangerous piece of water—today's Deception Pass—or got sucked into it. Quimper named this narrow passageway to the east Boca de Flon. H. R. Wagner claims that Quimper named Deception Pass after a Mexican general, but that is not likely, since the name is spelled wrong. The correct spelling should be "Flan," a word meaning "pudding" that is used in a number of phrases that mean "to shake like a pudding." Boca de Flan or Deception Pass is a fast and churning stretch of water for someone in any size of boat, a scary place—"like a small dog seeing a big dog, he starts shaking." This narrow passageway between today's Whidbey Island and Fidalgo Island bubbles and churns with whorl pools everywhere. On the north side of the passage are high rocky cliffs with a great view down into the deep gorge of the restricted waterway. Quimper's two explorers in their small craft were either sucked into Boca de Flan on the flood tide or were close enough that it scared the hell out of them. Thus, the Spanish name "Flan."

Lopes de Haro and Juan Carrasco waited for the slack tide to cross Boca de Flan, then headed north toward the southern end of Boca de Fidalgo or today's Rosario Strait. Once there, they had a choice to make to search behind the islands to the east and may have split up. One explorer went north and then east through the Bellingham channel. The other explorer went east into the Guemes Channel and then north. Whatever channels they used, they both ended up in Bellingham Bay, Drake's Bay. When they entered the bay on the flood tide, with line after line of small riptides pushing their small boats, they passed by the southern tip of the island shown on the Portus Map. Along this course they made a discovery. High on a point to their right, they spotted a large sun-bleached post, Drake's "great and firm post," on Post Point. As they drew near the landmark, they saw Drake's monument carved into the cliff face and recognized who had been there 200 years before.

When the two explorers reported back to the *Princesa Real*, Quimper then sailed the English ship north into Boca de Fidalgo, then east through the Bellingham channel and into Drake's Bay. He anchored his ship off Post Point and loaded kegs of powder onto the rowboat. His crew then placed the powder into a wave-cut cavity under Drake's monument, the same spot where Drake and his crew had signed their names. Above the carving high on the point, they broke Drake's "great and firm post" into pieces and threw the pieces over the cliff onto the beach. One piece of the post Quimper kept as proof that he had found Drake's Bay. His proof displayed inscriptions on "a plate fast nailed to the great and firm post." Then Quimper lit the fuse and set off the powder blast that echoed for miles. Drake's monument, of about three tons, broke loose and dropped straight down onto the beach. Pieces flew in all directions, one of which, a 100-pound chunk, landed about ten feet away. On this large piece of rock is Drake's sign of authority, the outline of his hand with a pointing index finger. As luck would have it, the imprint landed hand side up where it lies today, underwater at high tide.

With the discovery of Drake's Bay, Quimper also discovered a large sea to the north that he had no time to explore. What he saw to the north when he sail through the Bellingham channel toward Bellingham Bay was the lower Gulf of Georgia, which he thought could be the entrance to the Northwest Passage. He made charts of the whole area and then headed back out through the Bellingham channel to Boca de Fidalgo, "the entrance of the English gentleman who had gained knighthood through service to his country," the exit route of Francis Drake in the *Golden Hind*.

Francisco de Eliza had given Quimper two months to explore and then return to Nootka Sound. Quimper had been out only one month when his explorers found Drake's Bay, so according to his journal, he then held a meeting with his crew and they decided to head back out the strait. On his journey out, he followed the southern side of the Strait of Juan de Fuca, where he traded with local natives and got rid of the two canoes. At the outer entrance of the strait, Quimper discovered a good bay—Neah Bay—that Spain would later use and that would become a Spanish settlement. At this point, somewhere around the southern entrance to the Strait of Juan de Fuca, Quimper claimed the fog set in and he couldn't sail back to Nootka Sound. But the real reason why he didn't follow Eliza's orders is that Eliza would have taken credit for his discovery—Eliza was the commander in charge and had been born in Spain. Instead, Quimper headed south for Monterey, where he met

Salvador Fidalgo, who also decided not to return to Nootka Sound. From Monterey they both sailed back to San Blas, Mexico.

Eliza, at Nootka Sound, would not hear of Quimper's discoveries until the next year, 1791. Quimper would not return to the Pacific Northwest. Instead, he reported to the commandant of the marine department at San Blas, Bodega y Quadra, another Peruvian. Whatever the two Peruvians determined in their meeting, it didn't follow the chain of command. From the renamed English ship *Princesa Real* anchored in the harbor, Quimper wrote three short letters directly to the Viceroy, Revilla Gigedo, all on the same day, November 13th, 1790.

In the first letter Quimper confirms that he has delivered a box to the commissary, in which there are Indian arms, clothing, and other things found at the Strait of Juan de Fuca. This box really contained Quimper's proof of finding Drake's monument. Commandant Bodega y Quadra knew the importance of what was in the box, so he stood aside and let his fellow countryman take full credit for the discovery.

One important point about his first letter is that Quimper used the name "Juan de Fuca" for the strait he explored. This name originally came from the Englishman Michael Loc's story when he interviewed Juan the Greek in Italy in 1596. Then in 1787, English fur trader Charles W. Barkley sailed by the strait, and knowing of the Michael Loc story, he named it the Strait of Juan de Fuca. The Spanish had nothing to do with naming the strait. Spain knew that Juan the Greek really had named the strait Juan de Ulua, short for San Juan de Ulua, the location of their great victory over Drake and Hawkins. So the Englishmen, by naming the strait, helped the Spanish with their cover-up and sent historians down a dead-end road.

In Quimper's second letter to the Viceroy, written on the same day, he is asking indirectly that Lopez de Haro and Juan Carrasco be rewarded for their difficult efforts in the exploration—very unusual for just doing their job—so Lopes de Haro and Juan Carrasco discovered Drake's monument.

In Quimper's third letter, he confirms that he has turned over all the documentation of his voyage. Quimper turned over his documents to the commandant of the marine department, Bodega y Quadra, who will later negotiate with English Captain George Vancouver over the Nootka

Sound incident. So in November 1790, Commandant Bodega y Quadra knew the location of Drake's Bay. He also possessed all the charts made by Sub-Lieutenant Manuel Quimper. These charts not only showed Drake's Bay, but they also showed the entrance to a new sea, today the North Puget Sound, that could be the Northwest Passage. Spain then had confirmation from two sources that there could be a new route to the Atlantic Ocean. The first claim came from Juan the Greek in 1592, and now an observation made by Manuel Quimper in 1790.

About three weeks passed before Viceroy Revilla Gigedo wrote back to Quimper and confirmed that he received the box of Indian goods and that he would consider the reward for Quimper's two pilots, Lopes de Haro and Juan Carrasco. The Viceroy confirmed that he had received Quimper's proof that he had discovered Drake's Bay.

With Quimper's discoveries and the approval of the Viceroy, Spain immediately started to assemble another fleet to head back to the Pacific Northwest. At that time, Spain still held confiscated English property, and negotiations were going on between the two countries over the Nootka Sound incident. So, right amidst all the trouble with England, caused by Esteban Jose Martinez in 1789, Spain found Drake's Bay and a new sea that could be the Northwest Passage.

With these two important discoveries, Spain sent Manuel Quimper on a new assignment, to catch up with Alejandro Malaspina. Malaspina, an Italian in the Spanish Navy was on an around-the-world scientific expedition, and if on schedule planned to be in the Hawaiian Islands (at the time called the Sandwich Islands). Quimper, still using the English sloop *Princesa Real*, headed for Hawaii to locate Malaspina.

When Quimper reached his destination, he waited for Malaspina to show up, but Malaspina was way behind schedule, so while waiting, Quimper charted the Hawaiian Islands. While he was doing so, back at San Blas orders came from Spain to release all the English prisoners with full pay. In the *Argonaut*, after release, English Captain Colnett sailed back to Nootka Sound to find his other ship, the *Princes Royal*. Spain did not tell him they were using his ship, or where it was located. When Colnett could not find his ship at Nootka Sound, he finished his fur trading business and headed for Hawaii, and that is when the trouble started. In Hawaii, Colnett spotted his ship and confronted Manuel

Quimper. He wanted his ship back, and he wanted it back now. Quimper told him that he could pick up his ship in Macau, China, when Quimper was finished charting. In the heat of the argument between the two, Quimper started preparing for battle, and that forced Colnett to back down. Quimper finished his charting and then sailed for the Philippines, where he turned over the English ship. The *Princess Royal* was delivered to authorities at Macau, but a typhoon destroyed the English sloop and it was later sold for salvage.

Quimper, now in the Philippines, did catch up with Alejandro Malaspina, who just returned from exploring the Marianas. The two held a meeting where Quimper brought Malaspina's charts up to date with his discoveries in the Strait of Juan de Fuca. After the meeting Malaspina's orders were changed and he headed for the North Pacific. The meeting with Quimper happened on June 4th and Malaspina arrived in Alaska on June 27th, 1791. Malaspina's new orders were to search for the entrance to the new sea revealed first by Juan the Greek as a large lake and now by Manuel Quimper, after he discovered Drake's Bay. Manuel Quimper, after his meeting with Malaspina, headed back to San Blas, but the rest of his important story will continue later.

Spain Charts the Puget Sound

Spain approached Quimper's discoveries on two fronts. First, Malaspina headed north to Alaska and Eliza headed into the Strait of Juan de Fuca. As soon as Quimper departed San Blas to catch up with Allejandro Malaspina, Bodega y Quadra, commandant of the marine department at San Blas, organized another fleet back to Nootka Sound. When he received orders to release all Englishman and their crews with full pay, he still kept some of their property. He kept the 33-foot prefab schooner *Northwest America*. Martinez, in 1789, had dismantled the schooner at Nootka Sound and brought it to San Blas.

In 1791, the *Aranzazu* and the *San Carlos*, with the prefab English schooner loaded in the hold, headed back to Nootka Sound. Two important explorers were with the fleet. First there was Juan Carrasco, who along with Lopes de Haro had discovered Drake's Bay. Lopes de Haro did not return to Nootka Sound. The second explorer, Jose Maria Narvaez, had been with Martinez in 1789 when the English and American ships were confiscated at Nootka Sound. Narvaez, in 1789, had also sailed the English schooner *Northwest America* 60 miles into the Strait of Juan de Fuca to search for Drake's harbor, without success.

The fleet assembled by Bodega y Quadra arrived at Nootka Sound with sealed orders for Francisco de Eliza. One can only guess what the orders contained, and no doubt at that time, Eliza wanted to bring charges against Sub-Lieutenant Manuel Quimper. He hadn't followed orders and returned to Nootka Sound in August of 1790. But no charges were ever brought against Quimper, because Bodega y Quadra, his fellow countryman, outranked Eliza and protected him. The sealed orders that Eliza received are not known, but by following what Eliza did, we can infer what his orders contained. He first ordered the prefab English schooner *Northwest America* reassembled.

Eliza had been at Nootka Sound for over a year and likely wondered how he had got stuck in this hellhole. The winters are wet and cold, so his supply of biscuits had all molded. And even though barrels of lime juice had been sent north, most of his men were still sick from scurvy, or else were undisciplined and out chasing native women. Thirty-two soldiers and seamen needed to be sent back to California for recovery. Later, Eliza would be reprimanded by Viceroy Revila Gigedo for not doing his job—a hopeless task—which was to convert the local natives to Catholicism. At the time, the natives didn't trust the Spanish, because Martinez in 1789 had shot and killed their chief, Callicum.

As the Spaniards reassembled the *Northwest America*, Eliza, a married man who was far from home and lonesome, named the English schooner after his wife, *Santa Saturnina.* But his crew nicknamed the schooner *La Orcasitas*, after a barrio in Madrid, a low-class shantytown, meaning the schooner was a piece of junk.

Once the *Santa Saturnina* or the *La Orcasitas* was seaworthy, Eliza put Jose Maria Narvaez in charge, with Juan Carrasco second in command. Carrasco knew the route to Drake's Bay, but first—and what reveals Eliza's sealed orders—is that he wanted to know whether a shorter route existed to Quimper's new sea. So for the third time—first Narvaez, then Quimper, now Narvaez again—Spain re-explored every harbor indenting the west side of Vancouver Island. Only this last time, Eliza ordered Narvaez to follow each harbor to the end. As Narvaez did so, the native tribes whose territories he entered didn't appreciate his presence and attacked the *Santa Saturnina*. But before Narvaez retreated, he took note that the land rose high in the east and determined that it could not connect to another sea.

Eliza then sent the *San Carlos*, a pack boat, north to explore the terrain in and around Queen Charlotte Sound, but the ship returned. She had problems sailing in that direction. So Eliza traded ships and sent the *Aranzazu* north. He took command of the *San Carlos* and sailed her to the southeast end of Vancouver Island and anchored off today's Haro Strait. From there Eliza sent out a launch with explorer Juan Pantoja in charge. Pantoja headed north up the Haro Strait and made his way as far as the Saanich Peninsula. There, natives in brightly colored canoes attacked. Not wanting to fight his way past the natives or kill them, he retreated back to the *San Carlos* to wait for extra help from Narvaez in the *Santa Saturnina*, which hadn't yet finished exploring the harbors on the west side of Vancouver Island.

The route Pantoja had attempted to explore goes back to the voyage of Juan the Greek and the fictional voyage of Admiral de Fonté, which means that in Eliza's orders, Bodega y Quadra obtained the old charts of Juan the Greek, and that gave Eliza a place to start searching for the new sea. From the old Greek's charts, "he first sailed north, then northeast into a large lake." And that large lake, the lower Gulf of Georgia, is also what Quimper discovered when he charted the area around Drake's Bay.

When Narvaez arrived in the *Santa Saturnina*, the two vessels started out again. This time the natives didn't bother the Spaniards. The two vessels headed north up the Haro Strait, then northeast through Boundary Pass into the Greek's large lake, where they saw islands, just as the Greek had. The tides in Boundary Pass are extremely fast, so the Spaniards had to anchor and wait for the ebb. At times, with a good wind, the *Santa Saturnina* would tow the launch, until they reached the west side of the lower Gulf of Georgia. The two Spaniards made their way north up the gulf as far as Patos Island, where about ten miles away to the east they could see Drake's "white banks and cliffs that face the sea." To the north they could see a peninsula, Point Roberts, as was seen by

Juan the Greek when he entered his large lake. And to their north and northwest the two explorers saw Quimper's new sea that may connect to the Northwest Passage.

Patos Island is where the two Spaniards stopped. They then headed back to the *San Carlos*. On route, Pantoja noted that the tides in this new sea ran like a river, and at times they were surrounded by whorl pools. Once back at their ship, Pantoja told Eliza it would be a disaster to take the *San Carlos* through the route they had just explored. Pantoja also claimed to have named Quimper's new sea *Nuestra Senora del Rosario la Marinera.* Maybe Pantoja did name what is today's Gulf of Georgia, but likely with a little help from Francisco de Eliza, who knew Drake's history. Furthermore, this event of Pantoja naming today's Georgia Strait was written long after the fact—Narvaez had to explore the 138 miles to the northwest first. From Patos Island where the two explorers stopped, it is impossible to see what the Spaniards claimed. You can't see that far or where the waterways run. You would be lucky even on a clear day with the haze on the water to see 20 miles. So Pantoja's account was written much later, after Jose Maria Narvaez had explored the full extent of the Gulf of Georgia.

To understand what Pantoja's name for the Gulf of Georgia means, it needs to be broken down. The last part, *la Marinera*, is Our Lady of the Rosary of the Sailor; Spanish seamen refer to her as "the Sailor." And the *Nuestra Senora del Rosario* was the flagship for the Spanish Armada in the 1588 war with England.

In the 1588 war with England, the *Rosario* collided with another ship and lost her mast, then became separated from the rest of the armada. At the same time, Francis Drake was tracking the Spanish fleet and his orders were to guide the English ships with his stern lantern. When he spotted the crippled Spanish flagship, he abandoned his position, because he never followed orders, and captured the *Rosario* without firing a shot. Drake found the prize of the *Rosario* hard to resist and took the royal money chest she carried. So if "*la Marinera*" (the sailor) is pronounced first, what Pantoja projected in this name is, "the sailor who captured the *Rosario*." Furthermore, this is the same route taken by Francis Drake in the Gulf of Georgia or today's Georgia Strait to his first landing site at Birch Bay.

From where the *San Carlos* anchored near the Haro Strait, Eliza took the advice of Pantoja and did not attempt to sail through Boundary Pass. He moved the *San Carlos* farther east and anchored on the south side of the strait. With a copy of Quimper's charts, he anchored in today's Discovery Bay, an area protected from possible storms and also a great staging area.

Along the route that Eliza took to the southeast side of the strait, he skirted the San Juan Islands. These islands are the tops of a submerged mountain range. They range in size from big flat rocks to high-standing mountains. Some islands that face the strait are all windswept and have no foliage at all, a great landing spot for birds, who turn them white. Other islands are covered with giant fir and cedar trees. Eliza knew from the English publications that these were Drake's Islands of Saint James. So he assigned the name *Isla y Archiepelago de San Juan.*

The San Juan Islands

From *Washington State Place Names*: "Eliza did not name the San Juan's for Juan de Fuca, He named the Archipelago for the Roman Catholic Saint, Juan Bautista. [Saint John the Baptist]."

From the *New World Encyclopedia*: "The name 'San Juan' was given to the San Juan Islands by the Spanish explorer Francisco de Eliza, who charted the islands in 1791, naming them Isla y Archipelago de San Juan. The expedition sailed under the authority of the Viceroy of Mexico, Juan Vicente de Guemes Padilla Horcasitas y Aguayo, 2nd Count of Revillagigedo, and Eliza named several places for him, including the San Juan Islands."

The above descriptions are not correct. Eliza named the San Juan Islands for the "Battle of San Juan," a victory over Sir Francis Drake and John Hawkins. At San Juan, Puerto Rico, in 1595, Drake and Hawkins attempted to commandeer Spanish treasure from a galleon that had broken down, but the Spanish moved the treasure inland for protection. In the heat of the battle, according to the Spanish, Sir John Hawkins succumbed to a cannonball aboard his ship. English forces that attempted to storm the beach at night took heavy casualties when a large fire broke out, making the Englishmen good targets for the Spanish gunners. With the death of his cousin, Sir John Hawkins, Drake's fleet sailed away into the Caribbean, where Drake also died, from dysentery, in 1596. Eliza used the Battle of San Juan and the defeat of Sir Francis Drake when he named the San Juan Islands.

The statement from *Washington State Place Names* that "the San Juan Islands were not named after Juan de Fuca" is correct, but the two names are connected. If the correct spelling is used, from the Michael Loc story about interviewing Juan the Greek in 1596, and "Juan de Fuca" is changed to "Juan de Ulua," short for San Juan de Ulua, then the "Battle of San Juan de Ulua" joins the "Battle of San Juan"—both Spanish victories over Francis Drake and John Hawkins.

While anchored at the southeast side of the strait, Eliza sent Narvaez in the *Santa Saturnina* to chart today's Gulf of Georgia. Eliza had two objectives; first, he wanted to know whether the Northwest Passage existed, and second, he wanted to know how Francis Drake had arrived in this country and found his hidden bay.

With Narvaez heading north through today's Rosario Strait to chart, Eliza, with Quimper's maps, headed for Drake's Bay in a launch. He wanted to observe Quimper's discoveries. The launch stayed a good distance away from Boca de Flan, a scary place—today's Deception Pass—and rowed on into Boca de Fidalgo, the entrance of the English gentlemen who gain knighthood through service to their country. When Eliza entered Drake's Bay, he did not chart or name any landmarks, because he used Quimper's charts. And Quimper was noted for his cartography. Nor did Eliza have any comments about today's Bellingham Bay. But he did name Drake's Bay "Seno de Gaston" at the top of a ledger.

Bosom of Gaston

After Eliza observed Drake's monument at Post Point, he named today's Bellingham Bay Seno de Gaston. *Seno* is an Arabic word that has more than one meaning when translated into Latin. It could mean breast–coastline open-shaped arc, or it could also mean breast–chest, particularly a woman's. In this case Eliza meant breast–chest—particularly a woman's.

What he saw at Drake's monument, which was now in pieces, was the large bosom of Katherine Parr carved in stone, still intact. Drake's Bay is not an open-shaped arc. Bancroft's study of the area stated that at one time the northern half of the bay, almost an open-shaped arc, was named Gaston, but the name later disappeared. Eliza then used the name *de* (of) *Gaston.*

Born in Spain, Eliza knew the name *Gaston* well. This name was historical news throughout Europe and referred to Francois Mansart (1598-1666), a French architect who did work for the Earl of Gaston. Mansart always had the grand plan, like Francis Drake, and started a lot of projects, even one for the Queen Mother. But as it turned out, he never finished them. So when Eliza used the name *Seno de Gaston*, he made the statement that Drake's bosom and grand plan for this country may have been started, but will never be finished, just like the architect Francois Mansart's grand plans were never finished.

Jose Maria Narvaez in the *Santa Saturnina* went on to chart Quimper's other discovery, the Gulf of Georgia, or as named today, the Georgia Strait. But when he finished, all his bay-by-bay descriptions and charts disappeared. What is known or reported is that Narvaez ran out of supplies and only charted to the western end of the Gulf of Georgia. While there, he spotted whales and knew there must be another entrance to the ocean farther north:

> Located on the northeast coast of Vancouver Island, Johnstone Strait is home to one of the largest resident Orca [killer whale] populations in the world. Each year the whales return to the area to feed on the abundant supply of salmon, and to rub their bellies on the smooth pebble ocean floor of Robson Bight (Michael Bigg) Marine Sanctuary. (InfoHub, "Pacific Orca")

The Orcas of the Johnstone Strait number approximately 200 whales in total, and they can be easily recognized by their distinctive black-and-white markings. They are divided into three distinct population: residents, transients, and offshores. Each of the distinct populations has its own unique differences in behavior and feeding patterns, as well as minor differences in appearance. From the seat of a kayak, Orca viewing is an unforgettable experience.

Orcas also hunt the Gulf of Georgia in the area of Drake's landing and at times hurl their bodies out of the sea with a splash of white water that can be seen for miles.

Something else is missing here: Eliza also had sent the *Aranzazu* north into Queen Charlotte Sound, so what did she find? Did she locate the northern entrance to the Puget Sound and send a launch south to explore?

Then both Eliza and Narvaez got sick and left the North Puget Sound. Juan Carrasco took over the *Santa Saturnina* and sailed her back to San Blas. Narvaez did discover Drake's route in Nova Albion, but what he discovered will not show up until later, in another Spanish voyage in 1792, by Galiano and Valdes. Their exploration will come later; but first, what happened to Manuel Quimper, who found Drake's Bay, and Alejandro Malaspina, who explored Alaskan waters?

Alejandro Malaspina

Alejandro Malaspina, an Italian, joined the Spanish Navy. He had read and admired the explorations of English Captain James Cook. He knew from Cook's writings that on his third voyage of exploration to the North Pacific, he did not discover the Northwest Passage. But after Malaspina's meeting with Manuel Quimper in the Philippines and the discovery of Quimper's new sea while charting Drake's Bay, he wanted to know if a cover-up had taken place or if Captain Cook had missed the entrance, as he did that of the Strait of Juan de Fuca. So Malaspina retraced Cook's explorations in Alaska. When he confirmed no entrance to the Northwest Passage, he sailed to Nootka Sound, where he spent a month, in 1791. While there he tried to settle bad feelings with the local natives, caused by Martinez in 1789 when he had shot and killed their chief. But mainly, he wanted to know the results of Eliza's expedition into the Strait of Juan de Fuca. Then, once he knew his services were no longer needed in the northern waters, he headed for San Blas, Mexico.

While in San Blas, Malaspina and Bodega y Quadra, commandant of the marine department, received a dispatch from Spain regarding the Nootka Convention. The orders stated that Bodega y Quadra and Captain

George Vancouver would meet at Nootka Sound in late 1792 to work out details of a property settlement claimed by the English fur trader, Captain John Mears. Something else in the dispatch sent panic through the marine department at San Blas: What England wanted Captain Vancouver to do is to search for the strait missed by Captain Cook in 1778 and, if found, chart it. Spain somehow had to mislead Vancouver, because England didn't recognize Spain's ownership of the North Pacific. And if Captain Vancouver discovered Drake's Bay, as they had done, then England would claim Drake's Nova Albion and that could mean war.

Scrambling to send another voyage north, Malaspina sailed to Acapulco, where he found two new schooners. Construction on the two schooners had just finished and no sea tests had taken place yet. Malaspina took control of the *Sutil* and the *Mexicana* and replaced the crews with his own trusted men, commanded by Galiano and Valdes. Malaspina gave them orders to intercept Captain Vancouver and keep him at Nootka Sound: Don't allow him to chart the strait. They needed to keep Drake's Bay secret.

To know where to sail, Galiano and Valdes used the charts of Manuel Quimper and the charts of the Eliza Expedition into the Strait of Juan de Fuca, all compiled at San Blas. The story of the voyage of the *Sutil y Mexicana* will continue shortly.

Malaspina then continued his voyage back to Spain. While in the Spanish colonies of the new world, he had gained insight into the problems and the rebellion against Spanish rule. After returning to Spain, he projected his thoughts that the colonies should be free to trade and handle their own affairs. Then Spain could create a central government located in Acapulco. Malaspina's opinion about the colonies, or maybe something else he said, didn't sit well with Spanish officials. Spain confiscated all of his journals, seven volumes of exploration, and sent him to prison from 1796 to 1802. Napoleon Bonaparte, in 1796, commanded the French Army in Italy. He took up Malaspina's misfortune and negotiated with Spain for his release. Malaspina's journals from 1789 to 1794 didn't see the light of day until the late 19th century. By then, many of his documents had gone missing and the rest had ended up scattered throughout the Spanish archives. Malaspina's journals for the Pacific

Northwest contained information similar to Captain Cook's discoveries, but also contained information about Francis Drake's Nova Albion, all of which disappeared.

Manuel Quimper

In 1790, after meeting with Alejandro Malaspina in the Philippines and sharing his discoveries in the Strait of Juan de Fuca, within N 48°, Quimper headed back to the navy department at San Blas. Once there, local officials promoted him from sub-lieutenant, as he was under Francisco de Eliza, to frigate commander. Then he was called to Spain on personal business. While there, authorities inducted him into the secret Order of Calatrava—they knighted him. But why did Spain knight Manuel Quimper? Because he used an English ship and found the monument of the most hated English corsair in Spanish history, Sir Francis Drake. Not only did Spain knight Manuel Quimper, as Queen Elizabeth I knighted Francis Drake, they appointed him Minster of the Treasury at Vera Cruz. In comparison, Francis Drake received a prestigious appointment as mayor of Plymouth. With the proof that Quimper had discovered Drake's monument, Spain was prompted to follow England's treatment of Francis Drake. But that isn't all; Drake and Quimper had more in common.

Both navigators lost all the documentation of their voyages. Elizabeth I took all of Francis Drake's logs, and they were never seen again. All of Manuel Quimper's maps and journals disappeared in a Peruvian uprising. Neither of them, after being knighted by their respective countries, fit into high society. At social events Drake received a snobbish over-the-shoulder glance. The upper-class officers of the British Admiralty didn't accept him either and only called on his services as a last resort. Manuel Quimper later in life became a writer, and in the introduction to his book *Islas Sandwich* states that he "was treated as an American in Spain and as a Spaniard in Peru." During their lifetimes, neither explorer received recognition or respect for their real discoveries, which have until now been hidden in the history of the past.

Whatever Manuel Quimper took as proof of finding Drake's monument in 1790 is likely framed or standing in the halls of the secret Order of the Calatrava or hidden in the archives of the Court of Madrid. Somewhere in Spain, Drake's claim to Nova Albion adorns a dusty corner or maybe even a private collection. Who knows?

Voyage of the Sutil Y Mexicana

In 1792, English and Spanish explorers met in the North Puget Sound. From a dispatch sent from Spain to San Blas, Alejandro Malaspina learned that England planned to send their representative to Nootka Sound to meet with the Spanish representative later in the same year. But something else in the dispatch panicked the Spanish: England wanted to search for the strait at N 48° missed by Captain Cook in 1778, and if found, chart it. Spain definitely didn't want the English to find Drake's Bay—that would blow up the Nootka negotiations and England could claim the whole country.

Malaspina was conferring with officials at San Blas when the dispatch from Spain arrived. He then sailed for Acapulco where he took control of two new schooners, the *Sutil* and the *Mexicana*. These new schooners had not even been sea tested yet. They looked identical, both 46 feet long; only the sails were different. The *Sutil* was brig-rigged. Malaspina replaced the crews assigned to the schooners with his own men and put commanders Galiano and Valdes in charge. Their mission was to intercept the Englishmen before they could chart the Puget Sound and to take any actions necessary to keep Drake's Bay secret. But English Captain George Vancouver arrived in the Pacific Northwest early. He didn't report to Nootka Sound. Instead, he found the Strait of Juan de Fuca and started charting.

Meanwhile, the two Spanish schooners heading north had big problems. One of the new schooners broke down and had to be towed. When the *Sutil y Mexicana* on their slow journey north finally arrived at Nootka Sound, one of the local natives reported having already seen two ships enter the strait about a month and a half earlier. Galiano wasn't happy and wanted to know why the Englishmen hadn't been detained. So the Spaniards rushed repairs to their schooner and headed for the strait. Galiano and Valdes, using the charts of Quimper and Eliza, first sailed to a newly discovered harbor, Neah Bay, near the entrance on the south side of the strait. From there they headed east into the Strait of Juan de Fuca hunting English ships.

The *Sutil y Mexicana* would meet up with Captain George Vancouver in the North Puget Sound right where Drake first landed. But they had spotted the English ships long before that and had tracked them as they passed the entrance to Drake's Bay. Galiano and Valdes meet the English in the next chapter, on the Vancouver Expedition.

10

The Vancouver Expedition of 1792

Captain George Vancouver volunteered to sail to Nootka Sound to settle English property claims as agreed on in the Nootka Convention. Spain, in 1789, had seized English fur trading vessels and property at Nootka Sound. The property issue, regarding Royal Captain John Meares' claim that he had obtained land from the local chief and set up a trading post, needed to be settled in person. Captain Vancouver had been to Nootka Sound before, in 1778, as midshipman on Captain Cook's third voyage of exploration to the Pacific Northwest. At that time, as Cook's ships moved up the northwest coast, storms pushed them out to sea before they landed at Nootka Sound. Captain Cook missed the entrance to the Strait of Juan de Fuca, within N 48°. But word spread back to England from fur trader Royal Navy Captain John Meares that a strait existed to the east.

Meares claimed to have named the strait Juan de Fuca, from an old Michael Loc story, where Loc claimed to have met with the old navigator Juan the Greek in Italy in 1596. But Meares lied; he had heard the story from English fur trader Charles W. Barkley, who had sailed by the entrance in 1787 and named it from the Michael Loc story. When the Spanish heard the name the English were using for the strait, Juan de Fuca, they knew it was wrong, but they said nothing and just went along with it. Spain knew Juan the Greek had really named the strait Juan de Ulua, short for San Juan de Ulua, their victory over Francis Drake and John Hawkins.

Vancouver arrived in the Pacific Northwest about a month and a half early. He entered the strait in a new ship, HMS *Discovery* of 337 tons. His ship had the same name as Captain Cook's ship, but they were different ships. Along with the *Discovery* came a tender named the *Chatham*, of 135 tons, commanded by Captain William Robert Broughton. Along on the expedition was a surgeon and botanist, Archibald Menzies, who had also sailed to the Pacific Northwest before, aboard a fur trading vessel.

Vancouver knew contact would be made with the local natives, so he had procured pieces of copper and iron for gifts. As the expedition sailed along the southern shore heading into the strait, often times they saw canoes on the beach, but they observed no natives. Then again, the natives they did see paid no attention to them. Vancouver didn't know that Spanish explorers had preceded him by two years. He thought he was the first to have entered this waterway.

Deep into the 90-mile-long strait, Vancouver discovered a passageway to the south. He dared not take his ships where no explorers had sailed before, so he ordered excursion craft made ready. He also ordered his crew to fully arm the craft after what they had observed on shore—they had spotted native heads impaled atop long poles planted on the beach. The native tribes that lived along the southern shore were at war with natives across the strait and had been fighting for centuries.

So with a cutter, along with launches with eight oars, the explorers headed south into Admiralty Inlet. Vancouver assigned each crew a grid area. Curious native tribes paddled out to meet and trade with the strangers, receiving pieces of iron or copper for salmonberries and fresh fish. At times, when canoes were spotted on shore with no sign of their occupants, the surveyors left gifts as a sign of goodwill. The natives they encountered on the exploration south were friendly, until Peter Puget landed near today's City of Tacoma, at the southern end of the sound.

All of Vancouver's surveyors had orders to take measurements of latitude and longitude on shore to get accurate readings. Peter Puget, while on shore at the southern end of the sound, encountered natives who started fixing their bows and arrows. At the same time other natives began arriving in canoes, and they too readied their weapons. Puget drew a line in the sand that they seemed to understand, but their aggressive behavior continued. The landing party felt the threat, so Puget ordered a small cannon mounted in the launch shot across the water. After the boom, the natives stood stunned for a moment, then got back in their

canoes and paddled away. Vancouver documented no other aggressive native behavior in the Puget Sound, but later, and farther north in
Behm Canal, Alaska, the Tlingit did attack the survey. This clash with
the northern natives no doubt stemmed from their history of encounters
with the Russians.

Heading back north, Peter Puget in a launch and Joseph Whidbey
in the cutter traveled together while they charted their way along the
eastern shore of the largest island in Puget Sound, Whidbey Island.
Vancouver and Broughton both charted on the western side of the lower
sound. Captain Broughton finished his grid area about a week ahead
of Vancouver and moved the *Chatham* back into the eastern end of the
Strait of Juan de Fuca. There, he and botanist Menzies took a launch to
collect plants. While gone, the *Chatham* got caught in a fast tide in the
Bellingham Channel and lost the stern anchor. The crew tried to retrieve
the line several times and then figured the channel was a bad anchorage.
So they moved the ship farther north, to the west side of Cypress Island,
into Strawberry Bay. With the survey of the southern sound nearly finished, Captain Vancouver found that the work was moving too slowly
and issued these orders:

> On reflecting that the summer was now fast advancing, and
> that the slow progress of the vessels occasioned too much
> delay, I determined, rather than lose the advantages which the
> prevailing favorable weather now afforded for boat expedi-
> tions, to dispatch Mr. Puget in the launch, and Mr. Whidbey
> in the cutter, with a week's provision, in order that the shores
> should be immediately explored to the next intended station
> of the vessels, whither they would proceed as soon as cir-
> cumstances would allow. (Meany, *Vancouver's Discovery of
> Puget Sound*)

Peter Puget and Joseph Whidbey followed the eastern shoreline
north, between today's Whidbey Island and the mainland. They used
the ebb tide west through Deception Pass back into the eastern end of
the Strait of Juan de Fuca. Manuel Quimper two years earlier had named
this narrow passageway Boca de Flan, a scary place. With the *Chatham*
anchored within sight, in Strawberry Bay on the west side of Cypress

Island, and with orders from Captain Vancouver, Puget and Whidbey headed to the *Chatham* for provisions. They stayed for a short while and then headed back out to survey the islands east of their position. Strawberry Bay, where the *Chatham* anchored, is located in about the middle of today's Rosario Strait. Manuel Quimper in 1790 had named the Rosario Strait as Boca de Fidalgo, "entrance of the English gentleman who had gained knighthood through service to his country." He meant Francis Drake. The middle of the Rosario Strait was Drake's exit route from his hidden bay in the *Golden Hind*. The Bellingham Channel that Drake sailed through on route to the Rosario Strait and then out to the Strait of Juan de Fuca is the same channel where the *Chatham* had lost her stern anchor in a fast ebb tide.

At this point, one has to compare the journal of Captain Vancouver and the journal of botanist Archibald Menzies to find the route Peter Puget and Joseph Whidbey took to explore behind the islands to the east, in the area of Drake's Bay. From where the *Chatham* anchored, they headed back south and entered the Guemes Channel that runs east into Padilla Bay. There they met the mainland. The two surveyors followed the coastline north and spent the night on William Point, at the western tip of Samish Island. At this campsite one of the crew tried to chase down a small animal, but that turned out to have been a big mistake when the hot and heavy odor hit—they had met their first skunk. No way does that aroma wash off. It burned their noses and spread throughout the camp. This documented event implies that the smell stayed awhile and even hitched a ride north.

The next morning the surveyors continued east around Samish Bay and then north following the coastline. They passed the Chuckanut Formation, high sandstone mountains and cliffs pushed up from the seabed millions of years ago. As the two craft skirted the shoreline, they entered another large bay, Drake's Bay, about four miles from north to south and about the same east to west. At the southern entrance, the surveyors split up. Joseph Whidbey in the cutter headed north across the bay and Peter Puget in the launch headed east following the shoreline.

Captain Vancouver in his journal chose to leave out what happened next. We do know that Joseph Whidbey discovered a channel on the northwest side of the bay, today's Hale Passage. He could not follow this channel north because the flood tide pushed him into the bay, and he could not sail up the channel because a mountain on the island blocked the southeast wind. Joseph Whidbey would later enter Hale Passage using the ebb tide, as Francis Drake had done, from the north end to complete his charts. Captain Vancouver also left out what Peter Puget had charted in the bay and what he found as he skirted the southern shoreline.

As Peter Puget followed the shoreline east in the launch, he took his readings wherever he could find a good spot on land. Post Point is about halfway into the bay and is a great landing site. With the low daylight tides a gravel beach clearly stood out on the east side of Post Point. When Puget landed, straight ahead he noticed a large white section of cliff face different from the gray rock that surrounded the area. Two years before, when Manuel Quimper had blown Drake's monument off the cliff face, the blast had changed the color of the weathered wall rock. Then directly below the newly broken face, Peter Puget spotted the outline of two figures carved in stone. He saw Drake's creation in pieces on the beach, with 200 years less weathering than we see today.

While Puget and Whidbey were away exploring Drake's Bay, the *Chatham* departed Strawberry Bay and moved farther north up the Rosario Strait. Captain Vancouver, a week behind, then moved the *Discovery* into Strawberry Bay, but the season for the wild strawberries that Captain Broughton had discovered there had passed.

This is where a red flag went up. Edmond S. Meany, head of the Washington State Historical Society, wrote much of the early history for this area. He lost track of the timelines for the whereabouts of Captain Vancouver, Joseph Whidbey, and Peter Puget. Furthermore, he, and others, were completely baffled by the names Vancouver assigned for Drake's Bay. The names will come shortly, but first it is important to know where Vancouver, Puget, and Whidbey all were at this time. Mr. Meany claims that Vancouver was away in Canadian waters when Whidbey, alone, charted Bellingham Bay. His account is not correct.

Vancouver Names Drake's Landing

Both Peter Puget and Joseph Whidbey, after they charted Drake's Bay, followed the Bellingham Channel back to the *Discovery*, anchored in Strawberry Bay. The secret information they possessed could only be revealed to Captain Vancouver. Vancouver at the time had been correcting his readings for the area, and once he returned to the *Discovery*, they pulled anchor and headed north up the Rosario Strait, with Joseph Whidbey in the cutter leading the way. Peter Puget, on board the *Discovery*, then told Vancouver of his discovery behind the islands to the east.

On route up the Rosario Strait, Captain Vancouver claimed the survey in the south sound had taken too long and that they were behind schedule. So they would leave this broken-up land, the San Juan Islands, until later. He then met up with the *Chatham*, anchored at the northern end of the Rosario Strait, and both ships sailed into the lower Gulf of Georgia or the lower Georgia Strait. The two ships headed north to the next station, Birch Bay, Drake's "conuenient and fit harborough."

On route from the Rosario Strait to Birch Bay, Vancouver noted off his port side the long sandy beach at Lummi Bay. As they sailed north, both ships sailed past the high banks and cliffs of Drake's Nova Albion. So after they landed at Birch Bay, Captain Vancouver began to compile the pieces of the mystery of Drake's landing. To complete his information, Vancouver sent Whidbey back south in a launch. Along his route, Whidbey charted the high banks and cliffs all the way back south to Lummi Bay and found "Drake's Estro," where the Nooksack River entered the lower Gulf of Georgia. To complete his charts, Whidbey also needed to explore the channel that ran back south into Bellingham Bay through Hale Passage. During the same timeline, from Birch Bay, Captain Vancouver took Peter Puget with him in the cutter to chart north into Canadian waters. Once alone with Puget, he could get all the details of Drake's monument and the layout of Drake's Bay.

In his journal, Captain Vancouver left out the landmarks that could identify Drake's landing. He did give a brief description of the area when he described Bellingham Bay and Birch Bay, but not enough information to solve the old mystery. When Captain Vancouver compiled the charts of the lower Georgia Strait, he left out Joseph Whidbey's survey, where he charted "the white banks and cliffes, which lie toward the sea," and the sand spit at Drake's Estro, where Drake had trimmed the stolen *Los Reyes*.

Vancouver must have had a sixth sense while in Strawberry Bay, or maybe he spotted something, when he decided not to chart the broken-up land, the San Juan Islands, even though he already knew of Puget's discovery behind the islands to the east. Because out in the Strait of Juan de Fuca, a good distance away, Spanish explorers Galiano and Valdes in the *Sutil y Mexicana* were tracking his fleet up through the islands into the lower Gulf of Georgia.

Vancouver knew that Spain claimed this country and that negotiations with them at Nootka Sound were yet to come. He found himself in the same predicament as Sir Edward Bellingham had been in Northern Ireland. Bellingham's rule in Ireland faced Roman Catholic opposition after impossible reforms were imposed on the Irish by King Henry VIII. Captain Vancouver named Drake's Bay as Bellingham's Bay because Drake's monument represented King Henry VIII in a country claimed by Roman Catholics.

Bellingham's Bay

Edmond S. Meany, head of the Washington State Historical Society, wrote much of the local history in the area of Drake's landing, but his research found the wrong Bellingham—the correct person is Sir Edward Bellingham. This is what Meany wrote about Bellingham Bay, where he claims Captain Vancouver honored Sir William Bellingham:

> Sir William Bellingham. It is rather provoking to have Vancouver give this name in such an offhand way without indicating the man whom he sought thus to honor. Master Joseph Whidbey is the one who discovered and explored the bay while the Captain was away on his expedition to Texada Island. The Spanish chart by Elisa in 1791, as reproduced by Bancroft, shows the bay clearly enough, but it is given

no name, although Spanish names are sprinkled liberally on other places. Some have been retained, like the San Juan Archipelago, Guemes Island, Port Angeles, but most of them have been changed. Davidson's *Pacific Coast Pilot*, page 572, says that Elisa named this place Gaston Bay, but even that has now disappeared. Vancouver's name for Bellingham Bay has remained and what makes the name still more important, the fine city on the bay has recently assumed the name of Bellingham. There were formerly three cities, Whatcom, Sehome and Fairhaven. They have united under the one name. There was no one by the name of Bellingham on the muster books of the Vancouver expedition; but when they took on their stores and supplies on leaving England, their accounts were checked over and approved by Sir William Bellingham. He was thus one of the last administrative officers to come in contact with Vancouver and his officers. His office was controller of the storekeeper's accounts of his Majesty's Navy. It is claimed in Clowe's "Navy" that the office was discontinued on August 2, 1796. It is quite clear that this Bellingham is the one honored. Thus far no picture or biography of him has been discovered. (Meany, *Origin of Washington Geographic Names*)

Mr. Meany's argument has a few important and incorrect statements. First, Captain Vancouver was not away on his expedition to Texada Island while Joseph Whidbey charted Bellingham Bay. Vancouver was correcting his readings in the area and the *Discovery* was anchored in Strawberry Bay. And although Peter Puget is not mentioned, he was with Whidbey in Drake's Bay. The proof that the two were together is made in an earlier statement from Vancouver's journal.

Next, Francisco de Eliza never charted Bellingham Bay in 1791; he used Manuel Quimper's charts from 1790 and then they disappeared for 150 years. The Spanish map of the North Puget Sound and Vancouver Island supplied by H. R. Wagner in his book *Spanish Explorations in the Strait of Juan de Fuca* looks nothing like Drake's Bay, and the Spanish purposely drew it that way. Eliza named Drake's Bay as Seno de Gaston, written at the top of a ledger, without a map. And the map reproduced by Bancroft must have come from the Wilkes Expedition of 1847, that is where the northern half of the bay (*Seno*, an open shaped arc) had the name Gaston. But the "Seno" meant by Eliza was "breast-chest, particularly a woman's" after he saw the bosom of Katherine Parr at Post Point, a part of Drake's monument, discovered and blown off the cliff face by Manuel Quimper.

Furthermore, Meany found the wrong Bellingham. The correct person Captain Vancouver honored is Sir Edward Bellingham, who ruled for two years in Northern Ireland in the aftermath of King Henry VIII. And last, there were four settlements around Drake's Bay that grew together to become the City of Bellingham: Whatcom, New Whatcom, Sehome, and Fairhaven.

Washington State Place Names

Bellingham is a city on Bellingham Bay in Whatcom County. The first white man to enter the bay was the Spaniard Eliza in 1791, who named it Seño de Gaston or Gulf of Gaston. On June 11, 1792, the bay was surveyed by Joseph Whidbey in a boat excursion under Captain George Vancouver of the royal Navy. The latter, on receiving his officer's report, charted the name Bellingham Bay. He does not say for whom the name was given, but he frequently associated the surnames and Christian names of those honored by giving them to nearby or related geographic features. He gave the name of Point William to the prominent point south of the entrance to the bay. In studying his contemporaries, it was found that Sir William Bellingham checked over Vancouver's supplies and accounts as he was leaving England. There is very little doubt that Sir William Bellingham was the man thus honored. (Meany, *Origin of Washington Geographic Names*)

In the statement above, Mr. Meany claims that William Point has something to do with Vancouver naming Bellingham Bay. William Point is where Peter Puget and Joseph Whidbey camped overnight and one of the crew tried to catch a skunk. William Point on the western tip of Samish Island has nothing to do with the naming of Bellingham Bay. But it is interesting to know who he thought William Point was named for, because that too is wrong.

William Point

> The north point of Samish Island facing Samish Bay in north-west Skagit County is called William Point. It extends into Samish Bay marking the south entrance of Bellingham Bay in Whatcom County. Dionisio Galianeo named the point Punta de Solano in 1792. Later that year it was charted, as Point William, by Capt. George Vancouver, for Sir William Bellingham of the Royal Navy. (Meany, *Origin of Washington Geographic Names*)

Mr. Meany made an error in the statement above when he claims that later that year Vancouver charted William Point. Captain Vancouver's surveyors, Peter Puget and Joseph Whidbey, had charted the point before Dionisio Galianeo. At the time, Vancouver's ship was anchored in Strawberry Bay and then was moved to the next station in Birch Bay or Drake's "conuenient and fit harborough." Then came Dionisio Galianeo, after Vancouver. This timeline is important because it gives the route taken by the two Spanish schooners as they tracked the English ships and slipped into the Guemes Channel behind Vancouver to enter Drake's Bay. The English and Spanish ships at this point were only a few miles apart.

The Correct William

Captain Vancouver named William Point for William the Conqueror (Duke of Normandy) and his success at the Battle of Hastings, resulting in Norman control of England. After Puget and Whidbey left their campsite at William Point, they had charted Samish Bay next, where on the southern side of the bay they documented the Samish flats, a low swampy area and the entrance of the Samish River. This is not found in Vancouver's journal but is determined from knowledge of the area. When Captain Vancouver compiled this information, he associated the low swampy land with the Battle of Fulford: On the right flank was the River Ouse and on the left flank was the Fordland, a swampy area. This is where King Harold fought Harald Hardrada at Stamford Bridge and inflicted a decisive defeat on the Norsemen. Then barely had the Battle of Fulford finished when word came of the landing of William on the south coast, which prompted King Harold to march his battle-weary troops to meet William's army at Hastings, where on October 14, 1066, King Harold was killed and the Saxons decisively beaten. This is the William who Captain Vancouver honored when he named William Point—William the Bastard or William the Conqueror, who became King of England. So Mr. Meany's argument that Sir William Bellingham is the one Captain Vancouver honored is untrue.

When Captain Vancouver named Drake's Bay, he knew he was in Spanish-claimed territory, and he also knew of their hatred of Francis Drake and King Henry VIII. So with this knowledge, he handled the predicament as Sir Edward Bellingham had done in Ireland.

Sir Edward Bellingham

The Bellingham administration reached office in the summer of the year 1548; he was a soldier of approved vigor, showed that he understood the ancient animosity of the races to be revived, and now to be embittered by religious opposition. The English reformation, which King Henry VIII had imposed, had exhausted the only means that it possessed of recommending itself to the Irish. Bellingham governed for two years with Justice, without undue severity, but with the unflinching resolution of a man dependent on the sword, and earned the respect both of friends and enemies. By spreading the conviction of his unshaken firmness, he was able many times to try words before blows. (Dixon and Gee, *History of the Church of England*)

Captain Vancouver will later follow the example of Sir Edward Bellingham when dealing with the Spanish. After the discovery of Drake's Bay, he could have taken the whole country by force. His ships were well armed and it would have been a short battle. But as Sir Edward had done in Ireland, he used respect and firmness before blows. And through it all, he kept his discovery of Drake's Bay a secret.

After Vancouver named Drake's Bay as Bellingham's Bay, he left another clue, an important one. This name has been bounced around like a ball by historians, because no one knew who the name represented. Vancouver knew that Drake's monument on Post Point represented King Henry VIII, so he named the point of the peninsula directly across the bay, the tip of the peninsula shown on the Portus Map next to the island, as Point Francis.

Point Francis

Point Francis is at the west entrance to Bellingham Bay on Hale Passage across from Lummi Island in Whatcom County. In 1792, it was named by Capt. George Vancouver. In 1841, Cmdr. Charles Wilkes charted the feature as Point Frances. The U.S. Coast & Geodetic Survey later changed the name back to the spelling used by Vancouver. (U.S. Board of Geographic Names)

Sir William Bellingham was Controller of Storekeepers' Accounts for the Navy Board from 1790 to 1796. He then became a Commissioner of the Navy Board until 1803. His wife was called Frances. (*Washington, Oregon and California Place-Names*)

Captain Vancouver intended this name as a clue for us to figure out. But the Wilkes Expedition of 1841 changed Vancouver's spelling, and Edmond S. Meany found the wrong Bellingham, whose wife just happened to be named Frances. The correct person Vancouver honored in 1792, for Point Francis, is Sir Francis Drake.

Vancouver Names the Gulf of Georgia

This broad strait borders Whatcom County on the east, San Juan County on the west, and continues north between Vancouver Island and the British Columbia mainland. It is part of the inside channel of northwest Washington and southwest British Columbia. In 1791, it was named Grand Canal de Nuestra Senora del Rosario la Marinera by Francisco de Eliza. In 1792, it acquired the name Gulf of Georgia from Capt. George Vancouver, who honored King George III of England. Cmdr. Charles Wilkes confirmed that name in 1841 and the present variation has been approved by USBGN. (Washington Place Names Database)

The Gulf of Georgia is in the North Puget Sound and is also known today as the Georgia Strait. The question here is, if Captain Vancouver knew that Francis Drake had sailed into the Gulf of Georgia and landed in Birch Bay, his "conuenient and fit harborough," then how does the name connect to Francis Drake? "Georgia" does connect to Francis Drake, in a big way:

First, the word "George" means "tiller of land."

Second, the suffix "-ia" means "state of."

"Tiller of land" is no match with a body of water like the Gulf of Georgia.

But the "-ia"—the "state of"— could mean a condition or an assumption on which rests the validity or effect of something else. The "something else" is what Vancouver meant when he added the "-ia" to the name George.

Vancouver did not honor King George III of England when he named the Gulf of Georgia, and he did not honor himself. There is another George in this picture: Saint George, the patron saint of England. Francis Drake flew the flag of Saint George, a white flag with a red cross. Also, Captain Vancouver flew the Union Jack of England, which is a combination of the crosses of Saint George and Saint Andrew.

This is how Vancouver connected Saint George to Francis Drake. He used *The Golden Legend*, written by James of Voragine in 1265. The name "golden legend" does not refer to Saint George but to a whole collection of stories that were said to be worth their weight in gold. These stories popularized the legend of George and the Dragon.

Captain Vancouver knew that the Spanish called Francis Drake, "El Drague," the Dragon, because Saint George is also the patron saint of several towns and cities in Spain. These towns and cities belonged to the territories added to the old kingdoms of Castille, Leon and Aragon, during the "Reconquista." King Henry VIII's first wife was the Spanish Princess Catherine of Aragon, whose daughter, Mary I, "Bloody Mary," became Queen of England during Francis Drake's youth.

In Madrid, at the Museo del Prado, is a 14-foot-tall painting of George and the Dragon by Peter Paul Rubens, completed in 1620. At this intersection of both English and Spanish history, the common denominator is Saint George and the stories of the "golden legend." Vancouver recalled these stories from his boyhood and the passage that read, "The town had a pond, as large as a lake, where a plague-bearing dragon dwelled that envenomed all the countryside." When Captain Vancouver named the Gulf of Georgia, he used the "-ia" for the statement or stories of George and the Dragon. Drake's route was "as large as a lake," and his landing "envenomed all the countryside," Nova Albion.

Vancouver Names Birch Bay

Birch Bay, in United States territory, was named by Vancouver, in June, 1792, because a species of black birch was found growing on the surrounding shores in great abundance, the discovery of which was doubtless due to Vancouver's indefatigable botanist, Dr. Archibald Menzies. (Walbran, *British Columbia Coast Names*)

The black birch explanation is also given in the Washington Place Names Database.

When Captain Vancouver had decided to leave the charting of the San Juan Islands until later, he had known of Peter Puget's discovery behind the islands to the east. From the northern end of today's Rosario

Strait, he had headed north up the lower Gulf of Georgia to his next station, Birch Bay or Drake's "conuenient and fit harborough." On route, Vancouver saw a sand spit off his port side, where Drake had worked on the *Los Reyes.* To the northeast he saw "the white banks and cliffs, which lie toward the sea," of Drake's Nova Albion. At Birch Bay, Vancouver describes the surrounding landscape:

> This bay is formed by nearly perpendicular rocky cliffs, from whence the higher woodland country retires a considerable distance to the north eastward, leaving an extensive space of low land between it and the sea, separated from the high ground by a rivulet of fresh water that discharges itself at the bottom, or northern extremity of the bay. On the low land very luxuriant grass was produced, with wild rose, gooseberry, and other bushes in abundance. (Meany, *Vancouver's Discovery of Puget Sound*)

In another statement, Vancouver did claim there was black birch in abundance along the shore. But again, like he had used the "golden legend" when he named the Gulf of Georgia, he meant something else. Black birch has never grown in the Pacific Northwest. They only grow in the eastern United States. Paper birch does grow in the area, and one would think that Vancouver would know the distinct difference between the two, even though he wasn't a botanist. The black birch has bark more like that of a fir tree, brown and rough with deep grooves, and when one chops through the bark, the wood turns black. But the paper birch is white with black patches, smooth, with strips of the outer bark that peel off like paper.

Archibald Menzies, the botanist, also claimed black birch in his journal for Birch Bay. But the way he wrote the entry in his journal is questionable. What Menzies did is copy Vancouver's journals before they were published, because Menzies' journals still contained empty sections or missing parts that needed to be filled in.

Menzies and Vancouver were never on good terms, and each had kept his own journal. At the start of the voyage, Menzies was not under the control of Vancouver, but when the ship's surgeon got sick and Menzies agreed to take his place, he then came under the control of

Vancouver. That is when the trouble started between the two, which ended with Vancouver pressing charges against Menzies when they reached England. Vancouver also tried to claim Menzies' journals as property of the voyage. But Menzies had too many friends in the government, like Joseph Banks, the naturalist who had sailed with Captain Cook. So the charges were dismissed and Menzies kept his journals.

Back in England, Menzies had not completed his journals. He needed to fill in holes about the survey in the Puget Sound. While there, he had gleaned information from the crews when they returned to the ship. At times, he would go on excursions with Captain Broughton to collect plants, but he never asked Vancouver for any detailed information. When Vancouver's journals were released for publication, Menzies went through Vancouver's accounts and copied all his missing information.

While at Birch Bay, Menzies had walked through the bay and noted all the trees, like the poplars, but when he later saw Vancouver's entry about the black birch, he figured he had missed seeing them, so he added "and black birch" to his journal at the end of this entry. Menzies never saw the black birch at Birch Bay. And that is not the only place he made such an entry. When he noted the naming of the Puget Sound, he wrote, "which later became the Puget Sound." Not only did Menzies copy parts of Vancouver's journals, but before the journals were published, someone in the English Government replaced all the Spanish names used by Vancouver with English names.

What did Vancouver mean when he named Birch Bay? To understand why he used this name, one needs to know Captain Vancouver's personal history. He had gone to sea at the age of 15, and his naval education started while on Captain Cook's second voyage of exploration. While with Cook, he had a mentor, noted astronomer William Wales, and in his studies he learned that in pre-Christian Celtic society the Druids formed an intellectual class of philosophers, judges, educators, historians, doctors, seers, astronomers, and astrologers. To the ancient Druids, the birch represented "the tree of new beginnings and new perspectives," which prompted Vancouver to name a bay full of giant fir trees as Birch Bay. Vancouver knew that Drake had landed in this bay, and he used the "black birch in abundance along the shore" explicitly to note the character of the English hero. But at the same time, by using the name

Birch Bay, he tells us why he kept the discovery a secret: It was time for a new beginning and a new perspective, a time to bury Francis Drake.

English and Spanish Meet in the Puget Sound

Spain never did explore the south Puget Sound; all their efforts were north of the Strait of Juan de Fuca. Manuel Quimper charted the Strait of Juan de Fuca first and had found Drake's Bay in 1790. He saw today's Gulf of Georgia, but did not chart it. He headed back out the strait and then back to San Blas with his important find, plus proof of his discovery. Quimper's charts then passed to Francisco de Eliza, who sent Jose Maria Narvaez and Juan Carrasco to chart what is today Vancouver's Gulf of Georgia. These two Spanish explorers, in the names they assigned, used references to Francis Drake. Then at San Blas, right amidst the dispute with England and the Nootka Convention, Spain found out that the English were coming to settle property claims at Nootka Sound. They also found out the English were going to look for the strait missed by Captain Cook and if found, chart it. This sent panic through the naval base at San Blas, so Alejandro Malaspina urgently sent two of his trusted explorers, Galiano and Valdes, back north. These two Spanish explorers had the charts of Quimper and Eliza. Their orders were to do what was necessary to keep the English from finding Drake's Bay, and on Eliza's charts to change and rename any references to Francis Drake.

From Acapulco, Galiano and Valdes headed north to confront the English, but one of their schooners broke down and had to be towed. They were late arriving at Nootka Sound and angry when they received news that two English ships had entered the strait over a month before. After repairs were made, they sailed into the strait to hunt down the English ships.

The two Spaniards had never been in the strait before. So using their compiled charts, they first sailed to the south side of the strait to Neah Bay near the entrance. From there, they followed the southern shore, backtracking Quimper's exit from the strait in 1790. About 80 miles into the 90-mile-long strait, they spotted English sails at the eastern end of the strait, so they stopped and waited for them to move north into the

Gulf of Georgia. According to their charts, the English were near the entrance to Drake's Bay.

Captain Vancouver had just finished charting the southern sound and his ships were moving north up today's Rosario Strait into the Gulf of Georgia. The two Spaniards stayed at a distance until the English ships disappeared into the San Juan Islands. At that time, Vancouver knew of Peter Puget's discovery and made a decision to leave the charting of the San Juan Islands until later. So his two ships proceeded to the next station, Birch Bay.

Using Quimper's and Eliza's charts, Galiano and Valdes headed for Drake's Bay to see whether the English had discovered Drake's monument. With the English ships out of sight, they entered the Guemes Channel south of Drake's Bay, filling in missing areas on their charts. They followed the same route Joseph Whidbey and Peter Puget had taken about a week earlier. The two schooners sailed past William Point, into Samish Bay, and then north into Drake's Bay. Once they arrived at Post Point and observed Drake's monument on the beach, they had no idea whether the English had discovered the monument.

While the Spanish were following the eastern shoreline north to Drake's Bay, Whidbey had left Birch Bay in the launch and headed back south to chart Drake's Estro and the channel, Hale Passage, that ran north from Bellingham Bay. He had discovered the channel while in Drake's Bay but couldn't explore it, because the island on the Portus Map blocked the wind and the flood tide pushed his cutter east into the bay. The only way to chart Hale Passage was to use the ebb tide from the north, as Drake had done with the *Los Reyes* when he departed Sandy Point.

The timing of these two events was so close that the English and the Spanish almost met in Drake's Bay. Because a fast ebb tide runs through Hale Passage, it took Whidbey back into the bay; he then had to follow today's Rosario Strait on the west side of Lummi Island back north into the Gulf of Georgia. But as it turned out, the two parties never saw each other, and Whidbey with his charts of the Sandy Point area, headed back north to Birch Bay.

When the *Sutil y Mexicana* arrived in Drake's Bay and checked to see whether the English had discovered Drake's monument, they renamed the bay. While there, the Spaniards changed the name on Eliza's chart from Seno de Gaston to Bahia de Gaston. They also named the island shown on the Portus Map, today's Lummi Island.

Spanish Name Lummi Island

> Lummi Island, in Whatcom County southwest of Hale's passage, was charted by the Spanish explorers, Galiano and Valdes, in 1791, as "Isla de Pacheco," a part of the Mexican Viceroy's long name. (Roth, *History of Whatcom County*)

Local historian Lottie Roeder Roth surely meant 1792, because Galiano and Valdes were in Alaska under the command of Alejandro Malaspina in 1791. The viceroy's long name that Roth referred to is Juan Vicente Güemes Pacheco de Padilla, conde de Revillagigedo. But just because "Pacheco" happened to be in the viceroy's long name doesn't mean he is the person meant by Galiano and Valdes.

The correct name meant by Galiano and Valdes is López Pacheco, Viceroy of Mexico in 1642. When naming Lummi Island, the two Spaniards had made a statement. They knew that this was Drake's Bay and that Eliza had only named the bay and nothing else. So in naming Lummi Island, they compared López Pacheco with the destruction of Drake's monument. Viceroy Pacheco had been ousted from office for being in league with Portugal during the revolution against Spain. The statement they made by using the name Pacheco is that Francis Drake was also ousted, from Nova Albion when Quimper blew up his monument.

The Meeting

Once Galiano and Valdes finished inspecting Drake's Bay, unable to tell whether the English had discovered the broken-up monument, they caught the ebb tide out into the Rosario Strait, where they anchored to wait for the next flood tide. H. R. Wagner, in his book *Spanish Explorations in the Strait of Juan de Fuca*, thought the two Spanish schooners after leaving Bellingham Bay had sailed north up Hale Passage into the Gulf of Georgia. Wagner made a mistake, and that happened because he didn't know the winds and tides in the area. No ships sail north up Hale Passage. But Wagner did come close to solving the Drake's landing mystery. Through all his research and years of searching, he looked right at Drake's Bay and never made the connection.

The following morning, Whidbey, in the launch, spotted the two schooners off Point Roberts. He had no idea where they had come from and figured they had arrived during the night. He was right. The *Sutil* and the *Mexicana* had caught the flood tide in the Rosario Strait the night before and entered the Gulf of Georgia. And during the night they had passed the English ships anchored in Birch Bay.

Whidbey reported the schooners to Captain Broughton in the *Chatham*, and a launch was dispatched to meet with the Spaniards. Galiano spoke some English and told Captain Broughton, along with Archibald Menzies, that they were on follow-up charting under the direction of Alejandro Malaspina. In the meeting Galiano surely asked the Englishmen about their discoveries, but Menzies found the questions too insignificant to enter in his journal, or he referred any answers to come from Captain Vancouver. Plus Menzies had no answers to give. He didn't know Peter Puget had discovered Drake's Bay. So once the Spaniards found out where Vancouver was charting, they sailed north into Canadian waters.

At Spanish Bank, near Point Gray on the Canadian side of the border, Captain Vancouver and Peter Puget in the cutter spotted the *Sutil y Mexicana* at anchor. As they drew near, Vancouver noticed that they were flying the Spanish flag of war, and on board they spotted Spanish Special Forces. They were the 1st Free Company of Volunteers of Catalonia, wearing their black three-pointed hats with red rosettes and blue coats with yellow collars. These Special Forces were formed after the Spanish defeat by the British during the Seven Years War.

The two parties had a cordial meeting, and in their discussion Vancouver found out that one year earlier Spanish explorer Jose Maria Narvaez had charted far beyond where Vancouver had been exploring. This answered Vancouver's inner question, reported by Peter Puget, as to why Drake's monument was in pieces. The Spanish had discovered Drake's landing and blown up his monument.

Galiano's Chart, 1792.

After the meeting, the explorers agreed to meet again at Birch Bay, because Galiano and Valdes claimed they needed to fill in more on their charts. Once back at Birch Bay, now with Whidbey's charts of the lower Gulf of Georgia, Vancouver had all the pieces to Drake's landing. He personally had seen Drake's "white banks and cliffs which lie toward the sea" when he sailed from the Rosario Strait to Birch Bay. Then, from where Peter Puget had found Drake's monument to where Joseph Whidbey had charted the long sand spit and the estuary at Lummi Bay, Vancouver knew Drake's route. He knew Drake had entered Nova Albion from the north and not by the Strait of Juan de Fuca (Ulua). So while at Birch Bay, Vancouver knew that somewhere to the north there had to be another connection to the open ocean, and that is why he used the name "Gulf" of Georgia. From his knowledge, a gulf is a body of water between two straits, like the Gulf of Aden. In this case, the Johnstone Strait runs to the north and the Strait of Juan de Fuca runs to the west, with the Gulf of Georgia as an open body of water between the two straits.

When the Spanish met with the English again at Birch Bay, they exchanged charts of the area and agreed to explore together heading north. Both countries, hated enemies for centuries, knew about the dark shadow that lingered in Birch Bay but said nothing. Two English ships and two Spanish schooners, all anchored in Drake's "conuenient and fit harborough." We know Vancouver named Birch Bay, but what names did the Spanish assign for Birch Bay and Lummi Bay? Captain Vancouver had purposely left Lummi Bay and Drake's Estro off his charts.

Spanish Names for Birch Bay and Lummi Bay (Drake's Estro)

Lummi Bay, Drake's Estro (Estuary)

From the Washington Place Names Database (for Sandy Point): "In 1791, Francisco de Eliza called Lummi Bay, Punt de Loera, for Nicolas de Loera, a chaplain in the navy of Spain."

Another explanation: "Spanish explorers named the bay Ensenada de Loera or Ensenada de Locra. Spanish charts of Galiano and Valdes, dated 1792, used the latter name." (Washington Place Names Database)

When Galiano and Valdes entered the Gulf of Georgia at night in 1792, they passed the English ships anchored in Birch Bay, undetected. In doing so, they passed Lummi Bay or Drake's Estro during the night, at a distance of about a mile away. There is no evidence that they ever sailed back to the southeastern end of the Gulf of Georgia. They had used Eliza's charts from 1791, so they had no need to. But they did confirm Eliza's name for the bay, "Locra." Clearly, someone in Washington State history changed the spelling of the name to "Loera," a chaplain in the Spanish navy, when they couldn't figure out what "Locra" meant.

First, Lummi Bay was the entrance of the Nooksack River into the lower Gulf of Georgia until 1888, when a massive log jam changed its course into Bellingham Bay or Drake's Bay. The Nooksack River has always been the salmon fishery of the Lummi people, and still is today. But before the river changed course, the Lummi butchered all their fish along the shores of Drake's Estro. During the spring and summer when the majority of the salmon runs arrive, the natives were hard at work harvesting their winter food. At Lummi Bay in the summer, Drake's Estro is protected from the predominant winds from the southeast or southwest. There is no wind. So the smell of butchered fish just hung in the air.

In comparison, Lorca was a dangerous frontier town during the long struggle between the Moors who held Granada and the Christians of Castille. Lorca was also a large agriculture area that had a typical Mediterranean climate, with hot summers. The association between the Spanish name for Lummi Bay or Drake's Estro and Lorca is that Lorca had a lot of pig farms. The connection is the unpleasant odor of processing fish in Lummi Bay and the sweet smelling pig farms of Lorca.

Spanish Name for Birch Bay

When Galiano and Valdes reviewed Eliza's charts from 1791, they had no idea what he had meant when he named Birch Bay as Ensenada del Gamran, so they kept the name. To them, the name didn't relate to Francis Drake. But the named does connect to Drake. Eliza knew the name well, because he was born in Spain. This name referred to the nomadic tribes of Spain, the Magyars and the Gypsies. These tribes traveled from town to town, with the Magyars performing music and the Gypsies conveying mysticism. But both tribes always felt unjustly underpaid for their performances, so they would steal anything that wasn't fastened down.

The name Gamran came from the Gypsies, who were descendants of former inhabitants of India and were a problem not only in Spain but throughout Europe. In France, any second offense was punished by hanging. In the Netherlands, the Dutch completely kicked them out of their country. What "Ensenada [small bay] del [of the] Gamran [Gypsy association]" meant to Francisco de Eliza was "Bay of the Thief."

A local historian in the mid 1900's, schoolteacher Percival R. Jeffcott, saw Galiano's chart of 1792 and wondered what their name for Birch Bay meant. So, out of curiosity, he wrote a letter to Spain. He did receive a reply. The Spanish claimed the name should be Ensenada de Garzon, for a naval officer on one of the vessels. How the Spanish found the information after 150 years is unbelievable, but what is believable is that Spain knew that Francis Drake had landed in Birch Bay, and they had continued their cover-up.

In 1792, Galiano and Valdes also changed the Spanish name for the Gulf of Georgia. Eliza had named the gulf Nuestra Senora del Rosario la Marinera, "the sailor who captured the Rosario," which did identify Francis Drake, so they changed the name to Canal del Rosario.

From Birch Bay after their meeting and their exchange of charts, Captain Vancouver and Galiano and Valdes agreed to survey together. They started out to the next station, northwest into the Gulf of Georgia. But just past Point Roberts, the *Sutil y Mexicana* got swept away on a fast ebb tide into today's Active Pass. Both ended up in the Gulf Islands next to Vancouver Island 30 miles away. When the two met up again, the Spaniards decided not to stay with Vancouver's survey, because the ships could not sail at the same speed. So they went off to chart on their own. According to the Menzies journal, the two schooners stuck close to the survey all the way to the entrance of Discovery Passage, where James Johnstone made his way north to the open Pacific through today's Johnstone Strait. Once the Spaniards knew of Johnstone's discovery, they did leave the survey. But they would meet up again at Nootka Sound, where they would exchange more charts with Captain Vancouver.

Vancouver went on to chart Johnstone's newfound passageway to the open Pacific, for roughly 85 miles. His ships followed the eastern coast of Vancouver Island and used excursion craft to navigate up every side channel, but not without incident. At times they experienced gale-force winds and downpours of rain. And before their journey ended in Queen Charlotte Strait, both the *Discovery* and the *Chatham* grounded on rocks. But as luck would have it, at high tide they refloated their ships with little damage.

In Queen Charlotte Sound, the survey headed north until their charts matched those of Captain Cook, from 1778. In the back of his mind, Vancouver surely wondered how Francis Drake had found the lower inside passage and how far north he had really been over 200 years earlier.

The season started drawing to an end; the cold set in as the daylight hours waned. The time approached to meet with the Spanish representative at Nootka Sound to settle English claims, as stated in the Nootka Convention. But his survey in the Puget Sound was not finished. Vancouver left Drake's Islands of Saint James, the San Juan Islands, uncharted. He would later return to the area on follow-up charting. On his second trip to the inner waters, no Spanish ships would be there to track his survey. And he would have time to inspect Drake's Bay in person.

Negotiations of Two Powers

The problem to be solved at Nootka Sound stemmed from the fur trading post English Captain John Meares had set up there in 1789. Esteban José Martinez, in the same year, had seized all the property, along with

English and American ships. Martinez had then built a fort using the Chinese crew from the English vessels.

When the English ships reached Nootka Sound, they anchored at the entrance, in Friendly Cove. As the Spanish Commandant, Bodega y Quadra, arrived a full military greeting took place. Cannon salutes filled the air and sailors lined up on deck as a sign of respect for a visiting naval officer. Captain Vancouver as host served dinner with all the trimmings, and then negotiations began.

In several meetings, some hosted by Bodega y Quadra, some by Vancouver, the same ceremonial respect took place. While negotiating, they passed notes back and forth through an interpreter, but both men were firm in their countries' claims. They reached no settlement and referred questions back to their respective countries. Under the surface, both commanders knew but said nothing about who really had claimed this country, in 1579.

As the meetings took place, Bodega y Quadra and Captain Vancouver became friends. They both went to meet with the native chief, who entertained them in the local tradition, with dances and native cuisine. The two agreed that they should name this large island, John Drake's "largest and best," after themselves, and they called it Vancouver and Quadra Island.

With the return of the *Sutil y Mexicana* to Nootka Sound, they exchanged more charts of the area, and negotiations ended. One tentative agreement reached between the two was that Spain would move to the south side of the Strait of Juan de Fuca, to the harbor at Neah Bay, and the English would take over Nootka Sound. That is what happened. Then England and Spain would use the Strait of Juan de Fuca in common. The Nootka Conventions—all three of them—never reached any further agreement, and nothing was ever settled. England took over Vancouver and Quadra Island, but dropped the name Quadra. Spain did move to Neah Bay, but only stayed for two years, then packed up everything and moved back to Mexico.

In general, Captain Vancouver knew the Spanish were out of their element in the Pacific Northwest—the way they dressed, their food, and the way they lived. And no way could they protect such a large country from their home base in Mexico. When he observed 34 soldiers packed into each schooner, the *Sutil y Mexicana*, with everyone hardly able to move, he knew it was only a show of force and no real threat. But because of the person he was, a peacemaker, he treated his foe with respect, just as Sir Edward Bellingham had done in Ireland, and gained the respect of his enemies.

Captain Vancouver followed Bellingham's approach as a peacemaker, not only with the Spanish but also in Hawaii, where he spent the winter months. While there, he had an obsession to mediate a truce between the warring tribes of King Kamehameha and King Kahekili. Captain Cook had lost his life when he got between these two enemy tribes. Even back in England when asked whether on his survey he had seen any sign of Drake's landing, he replied no. Bringing up the past would only demean the progress he had made with Spain. Plus, England prevailed in her claims and acquired—without knowing it—Drake's Nova Albion.

Vancouver's Follow-Up Charting

After spending the winter in Hawaii, the survey headed back to the Pacific Northwest to continue charting from Alaska to California. In the Puget Sound, the San Juan Islands or Drake's Island of St. James still needed to be charted. This gave Vancouver a chance to inspect Drake's Bay.

The way Captain Vancouver describes Bellingham's Bay in his journal is more than he could have gleaned from compiling the drawings made by Joseph Whidbey and Peter Puget. He made comparisons that could only have come from first-hand observations.

Vancouver's Statement

The broken part of the coast that Mr. Whidbey had been employed in examining, was found to extend but a few miles to the northward of the spot where his former research had ended, forming altogether an extensive bay, which I have distinguished as Bellingham's Bay. It is situated behind a cluster of islands, from which a number of channels lead into it: Its greatest extent in a north and south direction, is from the latitude of 48° 36′ to 48° 48′; the longitude of its eastern extremity 237° 50′. It everywhere affords good and secure anchorage; opposite to its north point of entrance the shores are high and rocky, with detached rocks lying off it. Here was found a brook of most excellent water. To the north and south of these rocky cliffs the shores are less elevated, especially to the northward, where some of those beautiful verdant lawns were again presented to our view. Near the north entrance into this bay, the two Spanish vessels had been described by Mr. Whidbey, who returned, and communicated the intelligence to the ships: in consequence of which the *Chatham* weighed and spoke them off point Roberts, they having passed our ships during the night undiscovered. (Meany, *Vancouver's Discovery of Puget Sound*)

Most local historians assume that the "brook of most excellent water" Vancouver described is Whatcom Creek, at the east end of the bay. But there is another brook with crystal-clear water, between where Drake anchored his ship in Harris Bay and where his monument is located on Post Point. Padden Creek is easy to spot. It flows down the hill along the south side of the historic town of Old Fairhaven, over a large sandy flat, and into the bay, whereas Whatcom Creek is hard to spot. At that time, it flowed through the giant fir trees before entering the bay. Captain Henry Roeder and Captain Russell V. Peabody, who opened the first sawmill on Bellingham Bay, had to be shown its location by the Lummi Chief, Cha-wit-zit. So the *brook* referred to by Captain Vancouver is Padden Creek, where Francis Drake replenished his water supply before starting his long journey back to England in his newly named Spanish ship, the *Golden Hind*.

Vancouver also noted that while in Drake's Bay, "some of those beautiful verdant lawns were again presented to our view." *Our view* means he was there, in Drake's Bay. Peter Puget and Joseph Whidbey had presented their discovery to Vancouver. The "verdant lawns" he saw were on the north side of the bay, today the Reservation of the Lummi Tribe.

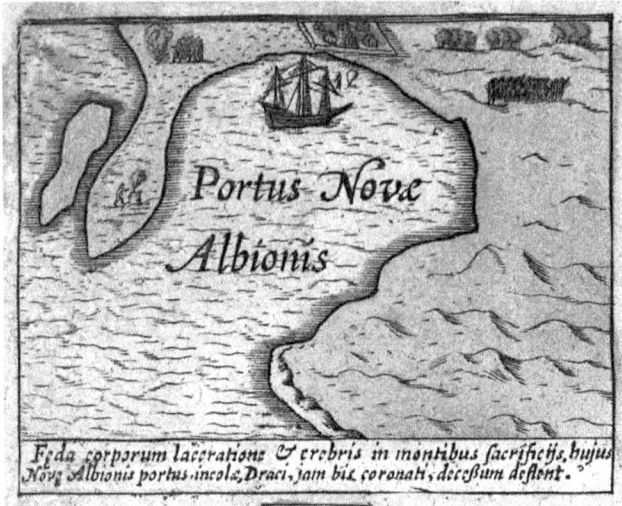

Judocus Hondius had copied the Portus Nova Albionis map.

The Portus Map does show three native huts just above the ship's mast on the north side of the bay.

"It everywhere affords good and secure anchorage." When Judocus Hondius had copied the Portus Map from the government buildings at Whitehall, in London, he had added the ship and centered it on the northern side of the bay, as a symbol. Drake never anchored the *Golden Hind* at that location in the bay; it is too shallow. He anchored in Harris Bay, on the south side of the bay. Then the day before leaving, Drake moved the *Golden Hind* out into the center of the bay and lined up his treasure-laden ship with the southwest channel before leaving early the following morning. The northern half of the bay is too shallow for all but a flat-bottom barge at high tide.

Captain Vancouver did travel to Drake's Bay on follow-up charting, and he did make first-hand observations. Only a few of his trusted surveyors knew of the discovery, and they kept the secret during their lifetimes. But all the clues Vancouver left behind in the names he assigned left a trail to follow, that he and his trusted crew did discover where Drake had landed.

Naming Puget Sound

Captain Vancouver did not say in his journal why he named the inland sea after Peter Puget. Washington State historian Edmond S. Meany claimed that only the area south of the Strait of Juan de Fuca should be named Puget Sound. He made his determination because that is the only place where Captain Vancouver documented the activity of Peter Puget. In the northern sound, Vancouver used the names New Hanover and New Georgia. Mr. Meany's interpretation is not correct, because when Captain Vancouver took possession of this country he claimed the whole inland sea as follows:

> From that part of New Albion, in the latitude of 39 20′ north, and longitude 236 26′ east, to the entrance of this inlet of the sea, said to be the supposed strait of Juan de Fuca; as likewise all the coast islands, ect. within the said straits, as well on the northern and on the southern shores; together with those situated in the interior sea we had discovered, extending from the said straits, in various directions, between the northwest, north, east, and southern quarters; which interior sea I have honored with the name of The gulf of Georgia, and the continent binding the said gulf, and extending southward to the 45th degree of north latitude, with that of New Georgia. (Meany, *Vancouver's Discovery of Puget Sound*)

When Captain Vancouver used the word "sound," as in Puget Sound, he meant a large ocean inlet, the whole Puget Sound, on both the north and the south sides of the Strait of Juan de Fuca. This inland sea is one ecologic system, today known as the Georgia Basin Ecosystem.

Vancouver honored Peter Puget because he had made the biggest discovery of the voyage. He had found Drake's monument in Bellingham's Bay, in Northwest Washington State.

All of Captain Vancouver's journals for publication were written after the fact, back in England, and released directly. On his charts he used many Spanish names in the North Puget Sound, but when the work was published, the Spanish names had all been replaced by English names. The Spanish, on the other hand, didn't publish their charts for 150 years, with Drake's Bay missing or not recognizable on the map supplied by H. R. Wagner.

Captain Vancouver volunteered to settle English claims at Nootka Sound and undertook what turned out to be the longest voyage of exploration in history, four and a half years. During his survey in the Puget Sound and from Alaska to California, he assigned over 400 names in six volumes. Because of his sickness, his brother John, with the help of Peter Puget, finished his last volume.

Captain Vancouver passed away young, at 40 years, as did his friend and counterpart in negotiations at Nootka Sound, Peruvian-born Bodega y Quadra. Both suffered the extreme conditions that had to be endured by explorers of the time. And both knew—and kept—the secret that, if revealed, would have led to a different history today. Captain Vancouver did one other thing that would ensure his cover-up of Drake's landing in the North Puget Sound and appease the Spanish. After he sailed south to the Royal Presidio of San Francisco and consulted with Spanish officials, he named the bay southeast of Point Reyes, at 38°, Drake's Bay. This cover-up of Drake's landing, by both England and Spain, has worked for over 200 years.

Now a third party arrived in Drake's Nova Albion: the Americans. They would change English and Spanish names and take possession of the bays where Drake had landed.

11

The Americans

Wilkes Expedition

B etween 1838 and 1842, the United States sent out an around-the-world scientific expedition. Spanish and British charts that had been acquired showed little detail that would be necessary for commerce, so many navigational areas needed to be re-charted. But at the same time, their fleet appeared to be a show of force, a new player on the world stage—and a powerful one. Included in the fleet were the 750-ton sloop-of-war *USS Vincennes*, the 650-ton *USS Peacock*, and the 230-ton brig *USS Porpoise*, along with two schooners, the 110-ton *Sea Gull* and the 96-ton *USS Flying Fish*. Charles Wilkes, in the introduction to his narrative of the *United States Exploring Expedition*, claimed, "The Expedition is not for conquest, but discovery."

In 1841, the American fleet explored the west coasts of South and North America, including the Strait of Juan de Fuca and the Puget Sound. In the area where Drake had landed, the Americans used English charts only, no Spanish charts. Here, one has to remember that England named the Strait of Juan de Fuca from the 1596 Michael Loc story about interviewing Juan the Greek, a navigator working for Spain in the Pacific. So at the time, for any waterway or point of interest not named on the English charts, Wilkes assigned an American name, as follows:

Area of Drake's Landing

- San Juan Islands (Drake's Islands of St. James):
  Navy Archipelago
- Rosario Strait (west side of the island on the Portus Map):
  Ringgold Channel
- Drake's Bay: Wilkes kept Vancouver's name—
  Bellingham's Bay
- Lummi Island (shown on the Portus Map):
  McLoughlin's Island
- Hale Passage (between the island and the peninsula on the
  Portus Map): named by Wilkes
- Sandy Point, at Lummi Bay (Drake's Estro): named by Wilkes
- Birch Bay (Drake's "conuenient and fit harborough"):
  Wilkes kept Vancouver's name
- Point Whitehorn, at Birch Bay (Drake's white cliffs):
  named by Wilkes.

Then starting around 1853, the United States Coast Survey tried to recapture the original Spanish names for the inner Puget Sound. So what we see today is a combination of Spanish names, Vancouver's names, and Wilkes' names. In some cases, the Coast Survey assigned Spanish names to places where there were no names. They did that to honor the first explorers, but the first explorers had nothing to do with naming them, like Eliza Island in Drake's Bay. Through all the naming and renaming of Drake's landing, not only were the Spanish names lost, but their correct meaning also disappeared. Galiano and Valdes in the *Sutil y Mexicana* in 1792 changed all of Francisco de Eliza's names that they thought were connected to Francis Drake. Captain Vancouver's names are still here today, but he left out the important areas, like Drake's *"estro"* at Sandy Point, and carefully worded his entries so as not to give away, without a great deal of research, Drake's lost North American landing.

Settling Drake's Nova Albion

When Peruvian Manuel Quimper entered the Strait of Juan de Fuca in 1790 and found Drake's monument, George Washington held the office of president of the United States. But the Americans were on a westward move toward the Pacific. In doing so, they had the English on the north, the Spanish on the south, and Native Americans in the middle. In the Adams Onis Treaty of 1819, Spain gave up to the United States their claims to the Oregon Country. Then the Oregon Treaty of 1846 between the United States and England establish a boundary on the 49th parallel. But England kept Vancouver Island, whose southern tip is within N 48°. With the Spanish out of the picture and boundaries set with England, everything seemed to be settled, but in 1859, a dispute broke out that almost started another war.

The dispute started over Drake's Islands of Saint James, the San Juan Islands. England needed a route from the 49th parallel through the Puget Sound to the open ocean. When the Americans inherited the Spanish claims, the agreement between England and the United States defined the boundary line between the islands as the deepest channel from the 49th parallel. England claimed today's Rosario Strait, along the west side of the island shown on the Portus Map, as the deepest channel. The Americans claimed the Haro Strait, at the southeast tip of Vancouver Island, as the correct channel. In the meantime, settlers from both countries had moved onto San Juan Island, which overlooks the Haro Strait and the Strait of Juan de Fuca. Both sides claimed the right to San Juan Island and figured their countries would back them up.

Then it happened: an American homesteader, Lyman Cutlar shot a pig that had wandered into his potato patch. The rooting swine belonged to Charles Griffin of the Hudson's Bay Company, who demanded that Cutlar be arrested. Accusations started flying back and forth as the incident began to snowball. But who had jurisdiction?

The American settlers demanded protection. In Drake's Bay, Bellingham Bay, the U.S. Army was constructing a fort on the east side of the bay. When the dispute broke out, all the troops were moved to San Juan Island. The protection came with the arrival of 66 soldiers of the 9th Infantry under the command of George E. Pickett. James Douglas,

Governor of British Columbia, in turn sent three warships commanded by Geoffrey Hornby to remove the Americans. Pickett refused to withdraw even though British forces outnumbered them.

Hornby wouldn't take action against the Americans without the approval of Rear Admiral Robert L. Baynes, who after arriving told Governor Douglas he refused to start a war over a squabble about a pig. At the height of the standoff over 2000 British troops with 70 cannons faced 450 Americans with 14 cannons dug in and ready for battle. If a fight had broken out, the odds seemed even, because 1500 of the British forces were not equipped to fight on the 55-square-mile island.

The potentially explosive standoff continued as President James Buchanan directed General Winfield Scott to contain the incident. Scott came to an agreement with Governor Douglas that each country should withdraw all but one company of troops until a solution could be reached. For the next 12 years, San Juan Island had a joint occupation of what is known as the English Camp of Royal Marines and the American Camp of the U.S. Army.

In the Treaty of Washington, between Great Britain and the United States, the question of the San Juan Islands went to a third party for settlement. Kaiser Wilhelm I of Germany, through an arbitration commission, determined in 1872 that the Americans owned the San Juan Islands. Half of Drake's Islands of Saint James then belong to the United States. England kept the Gulf Islands that lie to the north, with the Haro Strait as the deepest channel dividing the two countries. Out of all the islands in Drake's Nova Albion, well over 400 at high tide, England kept "the largest and the best," Vancouver Island, as stated in John Drake's second Spanish deposition made in Lima, Peru, in 1587.

The Gold Rush

Between 1856 and 1857, James Huston discovered gold near Fort Kamloops, on the Thompson River in British Columbia. Then a year later, a large placer discovery happened at Hill's Bar on the Frazer River. The Hudson Bay Company tried to keep all gold discoveries secret by buying all the gold. But when they sent a consignment to the San Francisco Mint, the cat was out of the bag and Canada had its first gold rush.

Thousands of Americans came through Drake's Bay and crossed the border using the Whatcom trail. As the gold dwindled on the Frazer River, prospectors made their way farther north to Cariboo country, where in 1859 a strike on Williams Creek brought thousands more. The early miners in their rush for riches took only the large gold and then moved on to better ground. Then Chinese miners followed and reworked the diggings by using mercury in the palm of their hands to extract the fine gold.

During the gold rush days, British Columbia was known as New Caledonia, and then later came to be called the Colony of British Columbia. To control the influx of immigrants with gold fever, Governor Douglas required all miners to get a license at Fort Victoria. But that didn't work with the miners who came through the Okanagan Country east of the Cascade Mountains, or by the Whatcom Trail north following the Frazer River.

At the time, rumors were flying that the lawless Americans would shoot any native on sight, as the 49ers did in California. So the Canadians tried to control firearms crossing the border, without success—the country was too large and their manpower too short. With all the restrictions put on American miners, most went home. But another gold rush between 1897 and 1901 in the Klondike again threatened Canadian territory, or so they thought, when a flood of Americans once again came through Drake's Bay and overran Vancouver Island waiting for passage to Alaska.

Owner of Drake's Third Landing Site

Daniel Jefferson Harris hailed from Patchogue, Long Island, New York, where after a family disagreement, he ended up on a whaling ship bound for the Pacific. He jumped ship in Hawaii, where he caught a ride to Victoria, B.C., and then arrived on Bellingham Bay, Drake's Bay, in 1853.

In need of a job, Dan Harris was befriended by John Thomas, who was the first to have acquired the property of Drake's landing, through the Oregon Land Law of 1850. Dan agreed to build a cabin on the beach near Padden Creek and proceeded to do so, but Thomas died before Dan finished the cabin. This sent his estate into probate. Dan finished the cabin and lived in it until finally, in 1861, he took over the Thomas land claim.

Dan Harris, better known as Dirty Dan Harris, in 1870, bought the 43 acres of Drake's third landing site in Bellingham Bay for $53.75 from Alonzo M. Poe. But he had to turn around in 1870 and buy it again for the same price, because Americus N. Poe, a brother, had sold it to A.A. Denny of Seattle.

"Dirty Dan" or "Grease Pot Dan" received his nickname because he never took a bath. No one called him that at the time, only after his death, because unlike Francis Drake, who stood five feet four inches, Dan towered to nearly six feet and weighed 200 pounds, very unusual for the time. Even the natives claimed you could smell him coming before you saw him; no doubt the bear grease he worked into his hair and rubbed on his body enhanced the aroma. He never shaved and most of the time displayed the same wardrobe: a top hat, unlaced work boots, and heavy trousers. When shorter residents got their chest-high view of Dan, they saw his unbuttoned red flannel underwear and his exposed hairy chest.

Dirty Dan Harris and Francis Drake had a lot in common. Both were entrepreneurs, independent minded, and they always had the grand plan. Dirty Dan refused to work in the sawmills or the coal mines, where most of the other men living on the bay worked. Instead, he had a side business. In his small sloop, he smuggled whiskey and rum at a time when no one sold booze to the natives. All of the tribes knew Dan, from Nootka Sound on the western side of Vancouver Island to Puyallup in the southern Puget Sound. His price was $1.00 a pint, but during the American Civil War the price went up.

Dan, like Drake, became a rich man, because of his under-the-table ventures, mostly whiskey, but he also lost money when he drove cattle into the mining district, as the starving miners had no gold. But he made it up later with the sale of prime property. Like Drake, rumors claim Dan had a stash, hidden booty, somewhere around old Fairhaven. With the lack of trust in banks of the time, where did prosperous people keep their money?

Today, Dirty Dan's profile sits on a bench in downtown Fairhaven, the small town he founded and named after the native word Seeseetichenl, "quiet place." But some residents think Dan doesn't deserve such an honor, because again like Francis Drake, he participated in the slave trade. Dan dealt in Chinese slaves when he moved to California, and Drake, with his cousin John Hawkins, had sold Africans to Spanish settlements in the new world.

There is little doubt that Alonzo Poe and Dan Harris saw Drake's monument at Post Point, but nothing is recorded. History in those early years was mostly by word of mouth. The scribes came later, after the fact. Early settlers around Drake's Bay passed stories down over a cup of tea or something stronger, somewhat like the local native history, until Charlotte "Lottie" Roeder Roth and Percival R. Jeffcott captured the stories on paper. This being the case, only the most outstanding events and characters around Drake's Bay were documented.

Local Historians

In recent years local historians have taken a stab at who made the rock carving at Post Point. An article in the *Whatcom Independent*, a weekly newspaper dated December–January 2005, claims that Spanish explorer Ferdinando Cortez discovered the Puget Sound around 1536 while searching for the Northwest Passage. He arrived with 21 ships and 700 men and built a fort at Post Point, on Bellingham Bay. The rock carving he constructed represented Adam and Eve and was meant to adorn the harbor. The article also claims that Cortez carried the stolen treasure of Montezuma, which he left behind in the fort when he sailed back to present-day Acapulco. After Cortez left, the local Nooksack tribe attacked the fort and entombed the Spaniards along with their treasure somewhere around Post Point. What a wild story, with a few flaws.

First, Bellingham Bay was Lummi territory, not Nooksack. The Nooksack tribe lived inland along the Nooksack River, but did collect shellfish on the tide flats of the bay. Both of these tribes were peaceful toward Europeans and only threatened to fight after the treatment they received from American miners during the gold rush years. Other raiding tribes from the north did prowl the area, but they never had the manpower or weapons to attack armed soldiers in a fort.

Second, if the old rock carving represented Adam and Eve, then why does Adam have his thumb in his right breast pocket? The carving represented King Henry VIII, carved in stone by the crew of Francis Drake.

Third, Cortez was never this far north and only spent a short time in what is now Lower California. As for having 21 ships, Spain didn't have the means to construct that many ships in the Pacific in 1536. Any maps the local historians may have to prove their discovery represent Lower California and not today's Puget Sound.

Fourth, their treasure statement could be right, but it did not belong to Cortez or come from Montezuma. Francis Drake is the culprit. From *The West Magazine* of 1965, Drake left tons of gold and jewels somewhere around his lost harbor. Is this another wild story? It is possible that Drake did leave a hidden stash of gold in Nova Albion, not tons, but a substantial amount, worth a lot of money today. Any tons would be silver, lost when his flagship, the *Pelican*, sank in the lower Gulf of Georgia somewhere around Birch Bay. And any buried gold and emeralds Drake may have hidden could be anywhere from Birch Bay to Bellingham Bay, about a 20-mile sail.

12

History Then and Now

As loggers felled the giant fir trees around Drake's Bay, small settlements grew together. The port drove black creosote pilings into the bay's floor to support floating boathouses and other buildings above the beach. Booms of logs covered the south side of the bay from where Drake anchored the *Golden Hind* in Harris Bay to the present-day City of Bellingham. Coal-burning ships spewed black smoke as they conducted commerce, loading cut sandstone blocks from a quarry on Chuckanut Mountain, cut lumber from the Roeder sawmill, and high-sulfur coal from mines whose tunnels ran out under the bay.

Commercial fishing added to the local economy of Drake's landing. In the early years, the late 1800's, after the Nooksack River changed course, fish traps were used on the northern side of Bellingham Bay, but they were later outlawed. When fish runs arrived in the summer, 50- foot purse seine boats worked the Gulf of Georgia during the day, while all sizes of gill-net boats drifted the waters at night. Now, in the present day, with the development of new fishing nets, all fishing is done during the daylight hours. Reef-netting, permanently anchored boats that fish on certain tides, is used in select places in the Puget Sound. Some fishing operations are no longer viable, like at Point Roberts, where native Semiahmoo intercepted salmon coming out of Boundary Bay. Some of the reef-netters that operate today fish the west side of Lummi Island, the island shown on the Portus Map. Dungeness crab fishermen string pots in the fall throughout Puget Sound, as draggers rake over the sea bottom, fishing cod, sole, and flounder. In the shallow bays, oysters and butter clam beds help support a rich fishing economy. As stated in *The World Encompassed 1628*, this country has all the needs of man.

Chinese played a big role in building the economy of Drake's landing, from building the railroad, completed in 1888, to working in coal mines and fish canneries. But as the need for their labor dwindled, the founding fathers decided they didn't want them around anymore. From stories told, they ran them out of town, and to make sure they didn't come back, a cable was strung around their houses, located along the railroad tracks, and a steam locomotive was used to tighten the loop. If one were to guess, these displaced refugees likely headed north to Canada, because the city of Vancouver has a large Asian population with great Chinese food.

From the boom and bust years of the past to present-day activities, the old buildings of Dirty Dan's Fairhaven have been refurbished. Sandblasters have cleaned the old brick to keep a taste of the past. Small shops and restaurants add flavor to a culture of immigrants that helped settle the Pacific Northwest.

In Old Fairhaven, down the hill toward the bay on Harris Avenue, the Alaska ferry is based where Drake anchored the *Golden Hind*, hidden from any possible Spanish ships. As the ferry heads north, it follows much of Drake's route. First it sails west into the Rosario Strait and follows the west side of the island shown on the Portus Map. Then it continues into the lower Gulf of Georgia. Once past the northern tip of Lummi Island, to the right is where Drake cleaned the bottom of the stolen *Los Reyes*, on the long sand spit at Sandy Point. Then for eight miles along the shore are the "white banks and cliffs that face the sea," to Birch Bay, Drake's "conuenient and fit harborough." Somewhere around Birch Bay the *Pelican* sank and first European contact was made with Native Americans, the Semiahmoo. The ferry then follows the Gulf of Georgia or Georgia Strait northwest for 138 miles to Discovery Pass, named after Captain Vancouver's ship, to the Johnstone Strait, ending in Queen Charlotte Strait. This is a trip worth taking, and it proves that Drake was a great navigator and knew how to keep his ships in deep water while sailing under overcast skies and in fog-shrouded waters.

Back at Old Fairhaven, driving east past the Alaska ferry landing at the bottom of Harris Avenue, ahead are the railroad tracks, and to the left is a small park, Marine Park, that overlooks Drake's Bay. Padden Creek, on the south side of the park, runs under a small railroad bridge and into the bay. This is where Drake replenished the *Golden Hind*'s water supply. This is where Captain George Vancouver found a brook "of most excellent water" while on follow-up charting to observe Drake's monument, discovered by Peter Puget.

Today, Drake's monument, about a quarter of a mile south following the railroad tracks from Marine Park, is hard to spot on Post Point; people walk right past it all the time and pay no attention. Four centuries of weathering has bleached the carving white, and the rain has erased the details. While trying to figure out why the three-ton carving ended up on the beach, my first thought was the big earthquake in 1700, a nine on the Richter Scale that dropped the Washington coastline ten feet, or maybe the railroad blasting their way through the point jolted it loose. But a closer inspection of the beach revealed broken pieces of sandstone with red copper stains, which confirms that someone blew it up—some pieces are too heavy and too far away from the carving to have broken off without the help of man. That is when the search for "who did it" began.

On a trip to Post Point a few summers back, off the point someone had dug a massive hole at low tide. With modern-day metal detectors one can guess why, because deep in the hole they exposed an old iron bed frame. The headboard of the bed had long thin rods with decorative round knobs, and it likely dated back to the 1930's. No treasure hidden in that hole, just an antique from the past. But there should have been a few butter clams to justify that much work. Later, an unnamed source said the hole was an archaeological dig.

If the hunt for Spanish treasure is still going on, then local historians or treasure hunters need to know the correct history. The old rock carving is English, not Spanish, and all the clues still sit on the beach at Post Point. And someone in England may have a map to the hidden cache, but they will need to know the correct location of where Drake landed. If Drake told Sir William Monson about sailing in a sea at 48°, then someone else, like Drake's brother Thomas or maybe one of the crew who dictated the *Anonymous Narrative*, may have drawn a map of the location. Because, once the Spanish departed Northern California and the United States became a country, two English ships showed up in San Francisco Bay hunting for the harbor of Francis Drake. Is this a clue for Drake's hidden treasure or, as they stated, did they just want to honor the spot?

All the research does suggest that Drake left treasure behind in Nova Albion. The main clue is that he sent his young cousin John with the Fenton Expedition, but in a small bark that could sail back through the San Juan Islands, to retrieve his fortune. But John's voyage with Fenton ended in disaster when his ship sank in Spanish territory. So whatever Drake hid is still where he left it, somewhere between three different bays in Nova Albion.

One would think that Drake marked the spot, a symbol on a boulder or rocks piled together, but time and weather have changed the landscape. Cliffs have collapsed, storms have smoothed the rocks, and logging has flattened the land. What this country looked like 400 years ago is lost. New, smaller trees now grow along his route, and beneath one of them is Drake's hidden stash. Someone digging one of these years may find a falcon of gold and emeralds as long as a man's finger, and wonder, who buried this? Francis Drake did, back in 1579.

Research

Wagner, H. R., *Sir Francis Drake's Voyage Around the World*, 1926.

In the preface to the 1955 bibliography of the publications of H. R. Wagner, Francis P. Farquhar wrote: "More than once Henry Wagner has remarked that his published works have never made a profit either for himself or for his publisher. They were designed for scholars in specialized fields and were not expected to be popular. That does not mean, however, that they are not important. As a matter of fact, many of them are so important that they will affect the writing of history for a long time to come" A true statement. (*The Published Writings of Henry R. Wagner*, Ward Ritchie Press, Los Angeles, 1955; Wagner Collection of Mexican Broadsides, www.library.yale.edu, 21 January 1998)

The used copy of this book that I ordered over the Internet had a previous owner's sticker in it, "Harold Gardner Bradbury." I looked up his name, and he turned out to be a hero in the Coast Guard, who in 1942 saved the crew of a burning ship. The pages have water stains. What an honor.

Academic Dictionaries and Encyclopedias, "History of the Church of England: From the Abolition of the Roman Jurisdiction," http://en.academic.ru/dic.nsf/enwiki/159907

Adams, William Henry Davenport, *Eminent Sailors*, Routledge, 1882.

Alegria, Ricardo E., *Discovery, Conquest and Colonization of Puerto Rico 1493-1599*, Coleccion De Estudios Puertorriquenos, 1971.

American Flag & Gift, "St. George's Flag," http://www.anyflag.com/history/stgeorge.htm

Anonymous Narrative, see Wagner, R. H., *Sir Francis Drake's Voyage Around the World.*

Answers.com, "Queen Charlotte Islands," http://www.answers.com/topic/queen-charlotte-islands

Archer, Christon I., "*Sutil and Mexicana*," Historica Canada, http://www.thecanadianencyclopedia.ca/en/article/sutil-and-mexicana

Bancroft, Hubert Howe, *The Works of Hubert Howe Bancroft*, http://www.archive.
org/stream/workshuberthowe27bancrich/workshuberthowe27bancrich_djvu.txt,

Barrow, John, *The Life, Voyages and Exploits of Admiral Sir Francis Drake*,
London, 1844.

Bartleby.com, "Sir Francis Drake Revived," http://www.bartleby.com/33/36.html

BBC, "Sir Francis Drake," http://www.bbc.co.uk/devon/discovering/famous/francis_
drake.shtml

BC Bookworld, "Bodega y Quadra, Juan Francisco,"
http://www.abcbookworld.com/view_author.php?id=3010

Blunderville, Thomas, reproduced in Wagner, R. H., *Sir Francis Drake's Voyage
Around the World.*

Bork, Janine M., "History of the Pacific Northwest: Oregon and Washington 1889,"
http://www.usgennet.org/usa/or/county/union1/1889vol1/
1889volumeIpage1-10.htm

Bourasaw, Noel V., "Introduction to Legends of Daniel J. Harris, His Character
and Accomplishments as Founder of Fairhaven," *Skagit River Journal of
History & Folklore*, 2007, http://www.skagitriverjournal.com/WA/Whatcom/
FairhavenSth/Harris/Dan01-Intro.html

Britain Express, "The Battle of Fulford," http://www.britainexpress.com/History/
battles/Fulford.htm

BritishColumbia.com, "History and Heritage of British Columbia, Canada,"
http://www.britishcolumbia.com/general/details.asp?id=22

BritishColumbia.com, "Langara Island, British Columbia, Canada,"
http://www.britishcolumbia.com/regions/towns/?townID=4006

Burland, Cottie, *North American Indian Mythology.* Barnes & Noble, 1996.

Canadian Encyclopedia, "Malaspina, Alejandro," http://www.canadianencyclopedia.
ca/PrinterFriendly.cfm?Params=A1ARTA0005052

"Captain Cook and the Spanish Explorers on the Coast," W. J. Langlois, Editor,
Sound Heritage, Vol. VII, No. 1, Province of British Columbia, 1978.

Captain Cook Society, "William Wales' First Voyage,"
http://www.captaincooksociety.com/home/detail/william-wales-first-voyage

Dictionary of Canadian Biography Online, "Vancouver, George,"
http://www.biographi.ca/en/bio/vancouver_george_4E.html

Dixon, Richard Watson, and Henry Gee, *History of the Church of England*, London,
1893, pp. 401-406.

Drage, Theodorus Swaine, *The Great Probability of a Northwest Passage*,
https://archive.org/details/greatprobability00drag

Drake Family Genealogy, "John Drake Son of Robert Drake (Brother of Edmund)," http://www.xroyvision.com.au/drake/library/early_records/records_9.html

Drake, Francis, "Sir Francis Drake on the California Coast," in *Early English and French Voyages, Chiefly from Hakluyt, 1534-1608*, Henry S. Burrage, editor, Charles Scribner's Sons, 1906; online facsimile edition at www.americanjourneys.org/aj-032

Drake, Francis, "Sir Francis Drake's Prayer," available at http://maggiesfarm.anotherdotcom.com/archives/1733-An-annual-re-post-Sir-Francis-Drakes-Prayer-1577.html

Drake, H. H., "Sir Francis Drake," *The Archaeological Journal*, Vol. 30, 1873; http://books.google.com

Enchanted Learning, "Explorers from 1501-1550: The Early Sixteenth Century," http://www.enchantedlearning.com/explorers/1500a.shtml

Enchanted Learning, "Explorers from 1551-1600: The Late Sixteenth Century," http://www.enchantedlearning.com/explorers/1500b.shtml

Encyclopaedia Britannica, "Seymour Narrows," http://www.britannica.com/eb/topic-537303/Seymour-Narrows

EnglishHistory.net, "Anne Boleyn," http://englishhistory.net/tudor/monarchs/boleyn.html

Essortment.com, "Amazing Exploits of Captain George Vancouver," http://www.essortment.com/amazing-exploits-captain-george-vancouver-25859.html

Fitzhugh, Edmund C., "The Nooksack War," http://search.tacomapubliclibrary.org/unsettling/unsettled.asp?load=Nooksack+War&f=indian.bat\nooksack.war

Gentlemen Adventurers, "Captain Sir William Monson," http://www.gentlemenadventurers.org/wmonson.htm

Georgia Strait Alliance, "About the Strait," http://www.georgiastrait.org/?q=node/44

Google Translate, "Our Lady of the Rosary La Marinera," http://translate.googleusercontent.com/translate_c?hl=en&prev=/search?q=Senora+del+Rosario+la+Marinera&hl=en&biw=819&bih=538&prmd=ivnso&rurl=translate.google.com&sl=es&u=http://nuestrasenoradelrosariolamarinera.blogspot.com/&usg=ALkJrhh3P6K1rIpti9V8u5KTqE1h-nWtxw

Grace Galleries, "John Meares," http://www.gracegalleries.com/Explorers.htm

Greaney, Michael, "How the Reformation Affected Ireland," http://www.humanities360.com/index.php/how-the-reformation-affected-ireland-59699

Hakluyt, Richard, *The Principal Navigations, Voyages, Traffiques and Discoveries of the English Nation*, 1589-1600.

Hayes, Derek, *Historical Atlas of the North Pacific: Maps of Discovery and Scientific Exploration 1500-2000*, Douglas & McIntyre Ltd., 2001.

HistoryLink.org, "Juan Perez and His Crew on Spanish Ship *Santiago* Sight and Name Mount Olympus," http://www.historylink.org/essays/output.cfm?file_id=5682

HistoryLink.org, "Mexican and Spanish Settlers Complete Neah Bay Settlement," http://www.historylink.org/essays/output.cfm?file_id=7953

Historylink.org, "Milestones for Washington State History," http://www.historylink.org/essays/output.cfm?file_id=5366

HistoryLink.org, "Whatcom County: Thumbnail History," http://www.historylink.org/essays/output.cfm?file_id=7327

HistoryLink.org, "Whatcom County: Thumbnail History," http://www.historylink.org/essays/output.cfm?file_id=7327

HistoryLink.org, "William I of England," http://www.historylink.org/essays/output.cfm?file_id=5682

Hodge, Cody, "The Relationship Between Church and State in the Middle Ages," http://www.humanities360.com/index.php/medieval-church-and-state-35027

In Drake's Wake, http://www.indrakeswake.co.uk

InfoHub, "Pacific Orca," http://www.infohub.com/vacation-packages-cb/10988.html

Island Vacation Rentals, "Lummi Island History," http://www.lummi-holidays.com/history

Johnson, Samuel, "Sir Francis Drake," http://www.readbookonline.net/readOnLine/36156

"Juan Perez' 1775 Visit to the NW Coast," http://www.hallman.org/indian/perez.html

Kelsey, Harry, *Sir Francis Drake The Queen's Pirate*, Yale University Press, 1998.

King's College, "Queen 'Bloody' Mary I Tudor of England," http://departments.kings.edu/womens_history/marytudor.html

Kraus, Hans P., *Sir Francis Drake: A Pictorial Biography*, http://www.loc.gov/rr/rarebook/catalog/drake/drake-home.html

Lamb, H. H., *Climate—Present, Past and Future*, Vol. 2, Methuen, London, 1977.

Luminarium: Anthology of English Literature, "Portraits of King Henry VIII," http://www.luminarium.org/renlit/henry8face.htm

Lummi Island Real Estate & Community Guide, "Lummi Island Ferry," http://lummiislandrealty.com/ferry.html

Meany, Edmond S., *History of the State of Washington*, 1909.

Meany, Edmond S., *Origin of Washington Geographic Names*, University of Washington Press, Seattle, 1923.

Meany, Edmond S., *Vancouver's Discovery of Puget Sound: Portraits and Biographies of the Men Honored in the Naming of Geographic Features of Northwestern America*, Macmillan, 1907.

Mendocino Community Network, "Francis Drake: California Summer Snow and Ice," http://www.mcn.org/2/oseeler/climate.htm

Menzies, Archibald, *Menzies' Journal of Vancouver's Voyage, April to October 1792*," edited by C. F. Newcombe, W. H. Cullin, Victoria, BC, 1923, www.openlibrary.org

Monroe, Felton, "Sir Francis Drake's Lost California Treasure," *The West Magazine*, July 1965, http://www.unz.org/Pub/TheWest-1965jul

Morgan, Carol H., "Elizabeth I of England," http://www.humanities360.com/index.php/biography-elizabeth-i-of-england-2-25065

Napier, Kimberly, "The Throckmorton Plot Against Queen Elizabeth I," http://www.helium.com/items/2410632-the-throckmorton-plot

National Maritime Museum, "Spanish Armada," http://www.nmm.ac.uk/server/show/conWebDoc.140

Needahand Spanish Properties, "Lorca," http://www.needahandspanishproperties.com/lorca.html

Nethelper, "Vancouver, George," http://www.nethelper.com/article/George_Vancouver

New World Encyclopedia, "San Juan Archipelago," http://www.newworldencyclopedia.org/entry/San_Juan_Islands

Nichols, Philip, *Sir Francis Drake Revived*, http://gutenberg.org/ebooks/2854

Northwest Citizen, "Please Tell Me a Dirty Dan Harris Story," http://www.nwcitizen.com/entry/please-tell-me-a-dirty-dan-harris-story?search=&category=44&author=

Northwest Digital Archives, "Guide to the Percival R. Jeffcott Papers 1870-1968," http://nwda.orbiscascade.org/ark:/80444/xv82087

Nuttall, Mrs. Zelia, *New Light on Drake*, Hakluyt Society, London, 1914.

Point Reyes Light, "Drake's 'Plate of Brasse' Proven a Hoax," http://www.ptreyeslight.com/stories/feb20_03/drake_plate.html

Pretty, Francis, *Famous Voyage*, 1589; reproduced in Wagner, H. R., *Sir Francis Drake's Voyage Around the World*.

Princeton University Library, "Pretended Voyages of Maldonado, De Fuca and De Fonté," http://libweb5.princeton.edu/visual_materials/maps/websites/northwest-passage/imaginary-voyages.htm

Princeton, BC, "History," http://town.princeton.bc.ca/history_of_princeton_and_area.php

Quicksilver.net, "Spanish Explorers," http://pages.quicksilver.net.nz/jcr/~vspanish1.html

Reading Borough Council, "Bayeux Tapestry," http://www.bayeuxtapestry.org.uk

Renaissance: The Elizabethan World, "Life in Elizabethan England: Religion," http://elizabethan.org/compendium/7.html

Rennard, Andy, "Giants and Tree Men," http://www.bfro.net/legends/salish.htm

Reveal, James L., "Menzies, Lambert, and Poiret," http://www.lewis-clark.org/content/content-article.asp?ArticleID=1509

RitchieWiki, "Fraser River Gold Rush," http://www.ritchiewiki.com/wiki/index.php/Fraser_River_Gold_Rush

Roberts, Rachel Pictor, "Medieval to Renaissance Period Changes in Culture," http://www.humanities360.com/index.php/medieval-and-renaissance-culture-25004

Rootsweb.com, "Birch Bay," http://www.rootsweb.com/~wawhatco/geog.htm

Roth, Lottie Roeder, "A Brief History of Washington State," from *History of Whatcom County*, Vol. 1, 1926; available at http://genealogytrails.com/wash/washingtonstate/history.html

Roth, Lottie Roeder, *History of Whatcom County*, 1926.

SamishIsland.net, "Historic Map," http://www.samishisland.net/si_historytimeline.html

SamishIsland.net, "Samish History Timeline," http://www.samishisland.net/si_historytimeline.html

Santosa, Alex, "Why Are Georgia (the State) and Georgia (the Country) Both Named Georgia?" http://www.neatorama.com/2008/08/18/why-are-georgia-the-state-and-georgia-the-country-both-named-georgia

Santschi, R. J., *Treasure Trails,* 1937.

"The Semiahmoo People of the Straits Salish," http://members.shaw.ca/j.a.brown/Semi.html

Shee-Eire, "Birch," http://www.shee-eire.com/Herbs,Trees&Fungi/Trees/Birch/Factsheet1.htm

Sol Boricua, "San Juan, Puerto Rico," http://solboricua.com/sanjuan.htm

Solar Navigator, "Sir Francis Drake," http://solarnavigator.net/history/francis_drake.htm

Sommerville, J. P., "Elizabeth I: Exploration & Foreign Policy," http://faculty.history.wisc.edu/sommerville/361/361-19.htm

Spate, O. H. K., "The Problem of Drake's Plan," *The Spanish Lake*, 2004; http://epress.anu.edu.au/spanish_lake/ch09s04.html

StandingStones.com, "Sir Francis Drake and Music," http://www.standingstones.com/fdrake.html

Tacoma Public Library, "Peter Puget on Puget's Sound," http://www2.tacomapubliclibrary.org/v2/nwroom/morgan/Puget.htm

Technische Universiteit Eindhoven, "Beyond the Map—Captains Galiano and Valdes," http://www.win.tue.nl/~engels/discovery/valdes.html

Telusplanet.net, "Early Years of the Canadian Northwest 1500-1599," http://www.telusplanet.net/public/dgarneau/B.C.1.htm

Telusplanet.net, "Early Years of the Canadian Northwest 1700-1789," http://www.telusplanet.net/dgarneau/B.C.3.htm

Thrower, Norman J. W., *Sir Francis Drake and the Famous Voyage: Essays*, University of California Press, 1984.

Tkachuck, Richard D., "The Little Ice Age," http://www.grisda.org/origins/10051.htm

Treasure Hunter's Insider, "The Lost Treasure of Ecuador," http://www.bc-alter.net/dfriesen/ecuador.html

Tudorhistory.org, "Katherine Parr" (Weidenfeld & Nicolson Archive), http://tudorhistory.org/parr/gallery.html

U.S. Army, "Catalonian Volunteers," http://huachuca-www.army.mil/History/Html/sanchez.html

U.S. Army, "Mexican and Spanish Settlers Complete Neah Bay Settlement in May 1792," http://huachuca-www.army.mil/History/Html/sanchez.html

U.S. Board on Geographic Names, "Point Francis," Docket 210, September 10, 1976; available at http://search.tacomapubliclibrary.org/wanames/wpnv2.asp

University of Victoria, "Potlatch," http://www.maltwood.uvic.ca/nwcp/central/resources.html

University of Victoria, "The Six Nations," http://www.maltwood.uvic.ca/nwcp/central/resources.html

University of Washington, "History and Literature of the Pacific Northwest," http://www.washington.edu/uwired/outreach/cspn/Website/Hist n Lit/Part Two/Texts/Juan de Fuca.html

U-S-History.com, "The Lummi Indian Nation," http://www.u-s-history.com/pages/h1556.html

Wagner, H. R., *Spanish Explorations in the Strait of Juan De Fuca*, 1933.

Walbran, John T., *British Columbia Coast Names*, 1909.

Washington Place Names Database, Tacoma Public Library, "Samish Bay," http://search.tacomapubliclibrary.org/wanames/dt6wpn.asp

"Washington, Oregon and California Place-Names: Point Francis," http://pages.quicksilver.net.nz/jcr/~vancouver6.html (accessed 2008).

Washington Place Names Database, Tacoma Public Library, "Georgia Strait," http://search.tacomapubliclibrary.org/wanames/dt6wpn.asp

Washington Place Names Database, Tacoma Public Library, "Juan De Fuca Strait," http://search.tacomapubliclibrary.org/wanames/dt6wpn.asp

Washington Place Names Database, Tacoma Public Library, "Lummi Bay," http://search.tacomapubliclibrary.org/wanames/dt6wpn.asp

Washington Place Names Database, Tacoma Public Library, "San Juan Islands," http://search.tacomapubliclibrary.org/wanames/dt6wpn.asp

Washington Place Names Database, Tacoma Public Library, "Sandy Point," http://search.tacomapubliclibrary.org/wanames/dt6wpn.asp

Washington Place Names Database, Tacoma Public Library, "William Point," http://search.tacomapubliclibrary.org/wanames/dt6wpn.asp

Washington State Historical Society, "Notorious Northwesterners," http://columbia.washingtonhistory.org/kids/spring2010/notoriousnwesterners.aspx

Washington State Parks, "Birch Bay State Park," http://www.parks.wa.gov/parkpage.asp?selectedpark=birch bay

Watson, Gary, "Henry VIII," http://www.humanities360.com/index.php/hnery-viii-england-protestantism-catholcism-biography-21058

Western Washington University, "Fairhaven & Southern Railway and Birth of the Two Sedros, Part 1," http://www.acadweb.wwu.edu/cpnws/centennial/people/harris.html

Western Washington University, "Welcome to Bellingham's Centennial: Exploring the Foundations of Our Community," http://www.acadweb.wwu.edu/cpnws/centennial/people/harris.html

Whatcom Independent, "Cortez Connection: Local Historians Examine Post Point Sculpture of Man, Woman," December-January 2005.

Whitfield, Peter, *Sir Francis Drake*, NYU Press, 2004.

Wikipedia, "Arica, Chile," http://en.wikipedia.org/wiki/Arica,_Chile

Wikipedia, "Fidalgo," http://en.wikipedia.org/wiki/Fidalgo

Wikipedia, "Francisco de Eliza," http://en.wikipedia.org/wiki/Francisco_de_eliza

Wikipedia, "Huguenots: The Calvinists of France," http://en.wikipedia.org/wiki/St_Bartholomew's_Day_Massacre

Wikipedia, "Johnstone Strait," http://en.wikipedia.org/wiki/Johnstone_Strait

Wikipedia, "José Maria Narvaez," http://en.wikipedia.org/wiki/Jos%C3%A9_Mar%C3%ADa_Narv%C3%A1ez

Wikipedia, "Juan Carrasco (Explorer)," http://en.wikipedia.org/wiki/Juan_Carrasco_(explorer)#cite_ref-pethick_1-2

Wikipedia, "Juan José Perez Hernandez," http://en.wikipedia.org/wiki/Juan_Jos%C3%A9_P%C3%A9rez_Hern%C3%A1ndez

Wikipedia, "King George's Sound Company," http://en.wikipedia.org/wiki/
King_George's_Sound_Company

Wikipedia, "Manuel Quimper," http://en.wikipedia.org/wiki/Manuel_Quimper

Wikipedia, "Manuel Quimper," http://en.wikipedia.org/wiki/Manuel_Quimper

Wikipedia, "Nootka Sound Incident," https://en.wikipedia.org/wiki/Nootka_Crisis

Wikipedia, "Ridolfi Plot," http://en.wikipedia.org/wiki/Ridolfi_plot

Wikipedia, "Rosario Strait," http://en.wikipedia.org/wiki/Rosario_Strait

Wikipedia, "Saint George and the Dragon" http://en.wikipedia.org/wiki/
Saint_George_and_the_Dragon

Wikipedia, "Seno," http://72.14.203.104/translate_c?hl=en&sl=it&u=http://
it.wikipedia.org/wiki/Seno&prev=/search?q=seno&start=10&hl=en&sa=N

Wikipedia, "Spanish Ship *Nuestra Senora de la Concepcion* (1570),"
http://en.wikipedia.org/wiki/
Nuestra_Se%C3%B1ora_de_la_Concepci%C3%B3n

Wikipedia, "The Tudor Conquest of Ireland," https://en.wikipedia.org/wiki/
Tudor_conquest_of_Ireland

Wikipedia, "Wilkes Expedition in the North Puget Sound," http://en.wikipedia.org/
wiki/United_States_Exploring_Expedition

Wilkes, Charles, *United States Exploring Expedition*, https://archive.org/stream/
narrativeunited10wilkgoog#page/n27/mode/2up

World Encompassed 1628, Library of Congress, Great Americana Series,
card number 66-26296, Redex Microprint Inc. (1966); also reproduced in
Wagner, H. R., *Sir Francis Drake's Voyage Around the World.*

About the Author

LAIRD L. NELSON was born in Bellingham, but grew up in the wheat country of Montana.

"I never knew the history of where I was born, so that stimulated my curiosity to find out. I have done many different jobs in my 72 years, from working at Boeing to a position as hotel manager, and then on to commercial fishing, but the hardest job was learning the discipline to write this book."